well-designed

well-designed

how to use empathy to create products people love

jon kolko

HARVARD BUSINESS REVIEW PRESS
BOSTON, MASSACHUSETTS

Library of Congress Cataloging-in-Publication Data

Kolko, Jon.
  Well-designed : how to use empathy to create products people love / Jon Kolko.
      pages cm
    ISBN 978-1-62527-479-3 (hardback)
  1. Product design. 2. New products. 3. Consumer behavior. 4. Marketing research. I. Title.
  TS171.4.K653 2014
    658.5—dc23

                                                                                2014032507

For Jess, my love and my best friend

contents

well-designed

introduction
from design thinking to design doing

It's hard to imagine a world without the simplicity of the iPad. But just a few short years ago, the clocks on our VCRs blinked the unset time, reminding all of us consumers of the encroaching complexity of modern technology in our homes and lives. The landscape has shifted radically and quickly, and we have changed with it. Since we're living in this landscape, it may seem as though we've collectively mastered the technology game, and that we just generally understand how to produce drop-dead simple products that tame the chaos of technological advancement.

But those of us who *build* products and services—those who are behind the facade of simplicity in the murky, muddy trenches of corporations, consultancies, and start-ups—are reminded of that complexity and confusion every day. Most of our product development processes are arcane and reflect outdated ways of thinking. The "product requirements document," for example—a leftover artifact from the 1980s—still seems to find its way into product development meetings, and those same meetings seem to spin endlessly around arguments about features, alignment, and time-to-market. As the market demands products that are simple to understand, robust in their technical capabilities, and most importantly, delightful to engage with, our legacy processes obviously don't deliver. And with consumer expectations relentlessly rising, becoming overwhelmed with the complexity of feature matrices and specifications is easy. In this increasingly complicated and pressurized world, it's hard enough delivering a useful product at all, much less one that someone really loves.

In the past decade, mostly in reaction to this anxiety and complexity, a number of methodologies have developed that purport to be fast, nimble, and quick. These methods reject documentation and deride linear process, swinging the pendulum in the direction of speed and results. Run loose and lean, it is said, in order to fail fast and succeed sooner. Yet these methods introduce a mess of their own, and as a result, consumers often end up with incomplete products that feel half-baked. While we can all take pride in shipping our products faster and more frequently, there is often real anxiety among both developers and marketers due to a lack of structure and process. "Agile? More like fragile," we mutter. In cultures that have embraced many of these new methods, it can feel as though the bus is moving at tremendous speed, but no one seems to be driving.

Now consider the company Nest, one of a select crop of companies that represents a sea change in consumer product development, producing amazing new products with what appears to be ease and confidence. Nest has produced an important innovation in heating and cooling—which might be the least exciting market segment ever—and its new "learning" thermostat has been described as "sexy" and "beautiful"; a CNET reviewer experienced "startling joy" using it.[1] In another conservative industry—finance—we find a payment app like Square, which is "one of the easiest and most fluid ways I've ever paid for something."[2] *Fast Company* lauded it as "both a foolproof and attractive experience."[3] In the hotel industry, Airbnb is turning hospitality on its side, with a simple, beautiful service-based product that changes the way we think about travel.

New products like these have launched in sectors as varied as health care, consumer electronics, financial management, and retail—and they have experienced large-scale growth and commercial success. Countless articles have described the brilliant user experience of products and services emerging from Apple, Nike, JetBlue, and Starbucks, and have correlated that experience with increases in profit.

The tiny, innovative Nest and its big and stodgy competitor Honeywell (130,000 employees) both have access to the same talent pools, to the same books and blogs, and to the same resources to help shape their products. So what was behind Google's acquisition of Nest for $3.2 *billion*? Why are Nest's products causing consumers and reviewers to use adjectives like "beautiful," "drop-dead gorgeous," "amazing," and "revolutionary"? How do companies like this make it look so easy, while the rest of us can sometimes struggle to get even the simplest set of features shipped in an elegant and effective way?

What makes these companies unique is that their products are the result of a *design process*, and it is this process that has led to unprecedented media fascination and consumer adoption. Modern start-ups like Airbnb and large corporations like JetBlue or Starbucks have proven that industry disruption is possible not by focusing on adding features or merely getting people to buy more, but instead by focusing on providing deep, meaningful engagement to the people who use their products or services. This engagement is achieved by designing products that seem as though they have a personality or even a soul. These products feel less like manufactured artifacts and more like good friends.

A NEW WAY OF DEVELOPING PRODUCTS

You may think of design as being about aesthetics or usability, and you may be familiar with design as it currently plays a role in your organization;

typically, the role is fairly insignificant, often fuzzy, and undertaken by a few people who are deemed "creative." While designers and developers may be asked to participate in brainstorming activities, their job is frequently prescribed for them: they are handed a specification and told to satisfy requirements that someone else has already defined. I've seen talented individual contributors scratching their heads about these requirements, because they are left without a strategic view of how these choices support larger business decisions. They don't understand why product decisions were made in the first place, and they question the value of particular decisions or an entire strategic approach.

While design has common connotations of aesthetics or ease of use, an important goal of this book is to get you to think of design less as a way of *making things look* a certain way, and more as a way of *getting things done*. The design process I'll lay out in upcoming chapters leads to innovation and emotionally engaging new products and services. This process is centered around *empathy* and is built on deep research with real people in their natural environments. It generates meaningful insights into human behavior and leverages these insights through a structured form of exploration. It is iterative, using visual thinking to explore potential possibilities for how the future will look. And it recognizes and celebrates creativity in *all* people involved in product development, not just the people who wear the black turtlenecks or horn-rimmed glasses. In fact, with the ongoing rise of digital technology and the general empowerment it provides to people in all kinds of enterprises, this design process and way of thinking applies to almost anyone involved in creating and providing products or services to customers, not just those already involved in product development or brand management.

In some of the companies mentioned, the word *design* is absent from job titles and process manifestos. But when you explore what the people at these companies are actually doing, it becomes clear that they are using the same methods and techniques as designers, as part of a comprehensive way of thinking about people and human behavior. In organizations that use this design thinking and process, product owners establish deep empathy with a community of consumers in order to identify problems to solve. They leverage a distinctive way of thinking in order to infer solutions to those problems that will have meaningful emotional appeal, and they align around a vision and a goal using shared visual artifacts.

At the core of design-focused product development is emotional engagement—the deep feelings a person forms about a product while using it. People tend to personify products—especially, increasingly, digital products—assigning them human characteristics and relating to them on an emotional, human level. To understand and design for this emotional appeal, it's critical not only to understand people, but to truly empathize with them in order to feel what they feel.

How can you can gain such genuine empathy? The only way is by spending time with people and getting to know them on a personal and intimate level, doing your best to see what they see and experience what they experience. This empathetic approach is designed specifically to generate *insights*, with an "insight" defined as a hypothesized guess about human behavior, but framed as a definitive truth. These insights hold the keys to innovation, and the clear, flexible design process described in this book provides the engine for developing insights into products people love, over and over again.

Put simply, in this book, you'll learn how to apply a powerful and repeatable design process to product management; when used effectively, this process will identify critical insights about people and will translate these insights into meaningful products.

Here are the four key elements of the process:

- *Determine a product-market fit*, by seeking signals from communities of users.
- *Identify behavioral insights*, by conducting ethnographic research.
- *Sketch a product strategy*, by synthesizing complex research data into simple insights.
- *Polish the product details*, using visual representations to simplify complex ideas.

This is an end-to-end process with specific, proven methods and techniques. Through successive chapters featuring instructive examples and lessons, as well as interviews with product managers for some of the world's best-known products and services, you'll learn how to shape and employ a process of design to develop your own engaging products. Specifically, you'll learn:

- That empathy is the key to building meaningful products, and empathy can be taught and learned.
- How to work through the complexity of human and qualitative research in order to arrive at the simplicity of a new offering.
- That a product's personality, which is critical to its success, can be established through a rigorous process of ideation.
- How to sketch visual representations that help communicate a vision of the future to a small team of cofounders or a large group of stakeholders.

THE NITTY-GRITTY

The book is organized around this design-led product development process, describing the entire path from idea to product execution. Here's a brief map of the book.

In chapter 1, I introduce design as a process built on deep, empathetic research with real people in their natural environments. This process generates meaningful insights into human behavior and leverages these insights to drive a creative process of exploration.

In chapter 2, I define product-market fit as the relationship a community of users will have with a product. I'll show you several frameworks for reflecting on the emotional needs communities have for your products and how to explore design-led market scenarios. You'll learn how to gather signals from a community of users, focusing on how their group interactions have developed and how the group, as a whole, behaves.

In chapter 3, you'll learn how to gain behavioral insights from your interactions with people. I lay out a method for conducting ethnographic research and show how to observe behavior that indicates hidden wants, needs, and desires in consumers in order to empathize with them. I also describe how to extract meaning from this behavior using a methodology called *synthesis and interpretation*, and you will see how this rigorous process leads to the development of core behavioral insights—of provocative statements of truth about human behavior that act as the driving force behind new product innovation and engaging design.

Once you've identified insights into human behavior, you can begin to translate those insights into a framework for a design strategy. Design strategy is a form of storytelling, and it emphasizes the unique stance your product takes. In chapter 4, you'll learn how to iterate through various emotional explorations in order to arrive at the perfect personality for your own product.

In chapter 5, I turn to product vision, describing techniques to craft the product and maintain control over the subtle emotional details. This includes mapping the product interactions, sketching the main paths through the interface, developing a visual aesthetic that supports a particular emotional goal, and—most importantly—helping the development team to see your vision for the future.

Finally, once your product has been designed, it needs to come to life. In chapter 6, I show how design must drive this task—typically an engineering activity—in order to release the right parts of the product at the right time and to ensure that the emotional integrity I've described is maintained. This means empowering developers to work toward a vision and providing them with a directional guide, or product road map, on the path to success.

While this book is built around a process and ultimately has a practical purpose—helping you to conceive, design, and produce better products—it is also making an important argument that has three main points: first, that designers can make great product leaders, and in fact that product leaders should have a design-focused sensibility; next, that nondesigners can easily adopt this design process and way of thinking, and that as digital technology becomes more universal, more people and companies will need to adopt it; and finally, that a design approach to product management is the most effective in both driving market fit and identifying behavioral insight.

Who is this book for? If you're already a practicing designer or product developer, you'll learn how to apply your existing skills in a new context and within a new framework that will help you gain greater effectiveness and clarity, increased control and productivity, and ultimately strategic influence and higher compensation.

If you are approaching product management from a different perspective—perhaps that of marketing and brand management—you'll learn how to appropriate a designer's stance, methodology, and process, and the deep value this brings in ensuring product-market fit. You'll learn how to view product decisions through the distinctive lens of design, asking and answering the question, "How does this particular decision positively affect the people who will use my product?" You'll also learn new methods and processes for managing a product strategy, the plan by which you'll achieve your product goals.

I hope, above all, that you find this book not just thoughtful but *actionable*, and that you'll apply this process in your own work, in shaping well-designed products that people love.

by design

It's 9:45 p.m. Joe McQuaid is sitting on the subway. He closes his eyes; he's thinking about the two-hour meeting he just had with his new boss. Joe is quitting his job and had just agreed to join a health and wellness start-up.

The opportunity is a good one, but Joe can't help feeling overwhelmed, and he hasn't even started yet. The company he is joining is well funded, but has been pursuing a dead-end path for the last six months. There has recently been a shake-up, complete with layoffs. Determined to pivot the company in a new direction, the management team regrouped with just four people and put out a plea for someone to run product development. Joe is that someone.

Joe's background is unique. He studied some engineering in college, but had always gravitated toward things that include people, not machines. His most recent role was as a senior interaction designer at a *Fortune*

500 financial company, and he is the first to admit that he doesn't have a brilliant health and wellness innovation just waiting to be unleashed. But the interview process went well, and he'd clicked with the team members. They trusted the approach he had laid out and were confident in his abilities. Tomorrow Joe will go to work as the chief product officer of a small start-up called LiveWell.

THE SCOPE OF A PRODUCT

Joe will be leading the product team, and we'll follow him as he moves into his new role and confronts the challenges of product leadership. But before we do that, let's try to understand what a product actually is.

Look at the objects that you have around you. You might be reading this book on a long-haul flight; you would be sitting in an uncomfortable chair with an armrest between you and the person next to you and a plastic water bottle in the seat-back pocket in front of you. You might be reading this book on a comfortable couch in your own house, with light from a good-sized reading lamp and a highball in your hand. All of these things are products: the couch, the lamp, the uncomfortable plane seat, the armrest, the water bottle, and even the plane itself. These products were envisioned, conceived of, produced, and distributed, and each object offers some value—utility, emotional resonance, or nostalgic memory.

Maybe you inherited the lamp from your grandmother, and each time you turn it on you remember her. Perhaps you purchased it cheaply, without much thought, at Target. While the executives at Target would love it if you fondly recalled your trip to their store, it's likely that the lamp serves only a utilitarian purpose: to provide light. Chances are good that you're reading a digital copy of this book on a digital device like a phone or an ebook reader. The idea of a product has become more confusing.

The phone is a physical object, just like the lamp. You might have purchased it, and it provides utility and value. But the physical presence of the phone is increasingly insignificant; it is simply a conduit for the presence of *digital* goods. It's highly unlikely that grandma gave you the phone, and it's even less likely that you remember her each time you turn it on, unless she appears on the phone's wallpaper image. In fact, it's unlikely that you paid for the phone at all. You probably received it for free from the phone company and haven't thought twice about it since.

If you didn't pay for the phone, and you attach no emotional significance to the object itself, your *ownership* of the *physical device* is increasingly insignificant. If you lost the phone, you probably would care much less about the plastic, metal, and glass of the object than you would about your digital photos, e-mail, and books contained *in* the object. In a digital world, data is the most important part, so the idea of a *product* becomes weird and amorphous.

If the phone itself isn't the product, what is? "The product" is the software application with which you access those photos or e-mails. Apple's iOS is a product, but since there's no chance that grandma gave you that, it's just as unlikely that you ever really think about it with emotional attachment. (Does anyone really "love" his or her operating system?) The software on the phone is divided into smaller apps that contribute value only when you use them. At this level of digital detail, you can start to feel something akin to an emotion, because these apps help you accomplish specific goals. When you *"like"* the photo of your friend's cat sitting in a cardboard box and looking smug, you are interacting with Facebook's mobile *product*. Your goal was emotional (to relate to your friends, or to have fun) or even more banal (to waste time). The Facebook product was designed to help you achieve those goals. It was also designed to help you achieve other goals that you didn't even know you had: to receive targeted advertising from companies, for example. Thanks, Facebook!

You can think of the web in the same way. It's made up of products that help you accomplish your goals. While Google is a big company, another way of thinking about it is as a series of applications, like mail, calendar, contacts, or groups. Each of those apps is an individual *product*, and each one likely has a *product manager*. From Reddit to the *New York Times*, you can start to consider digital goods as products, and if you look hard enough, you can find people who are responsible for both the vision and execution of each one of these products.

WAIT, THAT'S REALLY SOMEONE'S JOB?

Product managers are in charge of a product. That means they are responsible for identifying goals for that product, getting the product built, and then understanding if the product successfully meets those goals. In the world of analog "hard goods," product management is typically a marketing activity.

For example, product managers at Gillette might be in charge of a brand like Mach3, and would be called *brand managers*. They would identify market opportunities ("Other companies are offering razors with three blades!"), translate those opportunities into a set of product features ("We need more blades on our razor!"), work with other constituents to see the product produced ("Where can I source more blades?"), and then track how it performs in the market. They would be responsible for identifying which markets should receive the product, how much the product should cost, where it will be sold, and so on.

Product management, both in the context of a physical consumable and in the context of a digital product, is the process by which a product comes to life and the process by which it achieves and maintains success. It's not *project* management. That's a competency that's typically concerned with hitting a certain date or remaining under a certain budget, while remaining content agnostic. It's not product *advertising*; that's a competency that's typically concerned with how consumers learn that a product exists.

Instead, product managers become content experts, caring deeply about what the product does and how it does it. That doesn't mean they actually build the product. In the case of Gillette, a plastics engineer manufactures the shape of the handle or a chemist develops the special formula for the lotion in that little strip at the end of the hundreds of blades on the latest razor. In the case of software, engineers write lines of code to build the software. Product managers are responsible for articulating a vision for the product and ensuring that those who *do* build the product are working to achieve that vision.

That vision is about people and the market. **Product management is about ensuring a good fit between a product, a person, and the market.**

The fit between a product and the market depends on the relationship of competitive products and product accessories, the strategy for pricing and marketing the product, and the technological feasibility of building, distributing, and maintaining the product. Product-market fit generally takes and offers a macro view of the world and prepares you for thinking about concepts and strategies. It's about understanding what consumers, broadly, want, and what the market, broadly, will bear. Product-market fit is contextual to geographic region, time, cost, and execution.

The fit between a product and a person depends on the features included in the product, the emotions that are evoked by an experience with the product, the style of the product, the ease of integration between the product and other products, and the ability for the product to help a person achieve his or her goals (both utilitarian and aspirational). This fit generally takes and offers a micro view of the world and prepares you for details and tactics. The fit is about understanding what people specifically want, need, and desire.

WHAT IS DESIGN THINKING?

The traditional philosophical approach to product development emphasizes an outward focus on the market, on *what the competition is doing*. The tactics used to substantiate this philosophy are, unsurprisingly, marketing activities. These include market segmentation, e-mail marketing, advertising, focus groups, purchasing analysis, and competitive product launches.

With the advent of the internet, product management found a new owner: engineering. Companies with an extremely engineering-centric culture, like Microsoft or Google, naturally placed competent technologists in charge of developing not only the product but the *product strategy*. An engineering approach to product management emphasizes an inward focus on technology, on *what unique capabilities and features the team can build*. This technological approach doesn't ignore marketing activities. It simply sees the market through an engineering lens and places a higher priority on engineering activities. These activities typically include things like requirement definition, writing good code, creating public application program interfaces (APIs), optimization, quality assurance, feature development, and algorithms.

There's a third approach to product management, one that is rooted in design. The word "design" has typically been used to describe craftsmanship in furniture, aesthetics in posters, and the styling of physical products, like toasters or cars. Historically, designers made things look good. For many years, this made designers feel as though their contribution was superficial, as they would be called in when a product was nearly complete and asked to "just skin it." Now design aspires to be bigger than aesthetics. Designers describe their discipline as one of solving problems and view design as a critical process to go through in order to make sense of complexity and help humanize technology. The design process is commonly described as *user centered*, rather than *market or technology centered*, meaning that decisions are made in order to help people accomplish their goals and achieve their aspirations.

Recently, this process has been called *design thinking*, because the way designers think about problems can be viewed as a different way of thinking about the world. *Design thinking* is juxtaposed with *analytical thinking*. Designers learn to purposefully embrace intuitive or inferential leaps of logic, and to use sketching and drawing as a way of solving problems. For the purposes of this text, *design* and *design thinking* are used interchangeably. Both imply a "designerly" approach to solving problems.

Many large corporations have embraced *design* because it is a process that drives innovation and helps companies avoid the threat of commoditization. It's also discussed in the context of service complexity, as design can help manage organizational change, improve mission-critical services (such as health care), and even examine existing governmental policy in new ways.

That design can also be used effectively for product management is no surprise. Product managers who have a background in design typically pursue a product strategy that is *user centered*. When they make a decision, it's primarily in support of the people who will use the product, rather than in support of a business driver or a technological advancement. This doesn't mean that product management by design ignores technology or the realities of business. It simply places a priority on people, rather than prioritizing business or engineering, and uses this lens to resolve conflicts and prioritize decisions.

Consider how this stance plays out in a fairly typical product meeting between a technologist, a marketer, and the product manager:

Marketer: *We've got a series of banner ads set to kick off tomorrow to promote the new product. Is the release ready for launch?*

Engineer: *The release is feature complete, but I'll need an extra week to work on resolving some usability issues. However, the schedule shows that I'm supposed to move on to building some new functionality ASAP. Maybe these usability issues can wait. And also, banner ads suck.*

Marketer *[under his breath]: No, you suck.*

Sure, the example is overly simplistic. But it represents the *type* of conflict a product manager must resolve, and must resolve frequently. She could delay the launch of the product in order to focus on the usability issues, *prioritizing the user of the product over the internal schedule or the planned marketing efforts*. If she takes this course of action, she'll need to *deal with the repercussions of a delayed release*.

Or, she could delay the usability fixes and launch the product, *prioritizing the scheduling of development resources and marketing efforts over the user of the product*. If she takes this course of action, she'll need to *deal with the consequences of usability issues in her product*.

A product manager continually faces situations like this with regard to topics as vast as resourcing, cost, scheduling, quality, and features. Rarely is the choice as binary as presented here, as these decisions are highly contextual. Yet product management by design makes these decisions easier, because it provides a consistent perspective from which to analyze and consider decisions.

Because design is a philosophical way of thinking about product management that champions for the user, this manager decides in favor of the person who has to use the software. She then faces the consequences of a delayed release. She makes her priority a product that is as easy to use as possible rather than a product that launches on time or a product that is lush with features. She also breaks off the meeting, lest the banter about the value of banner ads leads to a fist fight.

Product management by design focuses on goals and emotions. Imagine that you are the product manager in the example. You've made a decision—to delay the release—and now you must face the consequences. Delay can often have a domino effect. It can disrupt other people's resourcing needs. It can have financial implications. Making a product decision from a perspective of ideology is either brave or stupid, so I want to carefully characterize *product management by design* as neither ideological nor dogmatic. In real life, product decisions are always complicated and constantly require compromise. But product management by design will *generally* pursue an agenda of users over technology or marketing, and the product manager will frequently find herself acting as a champion for people's wants, needs, and desires.

In a big organization, this approach is often a minority opinion and can be tedious. Holding up a release makes waves in any company, and those waves can be interpreted as troubling, as if they are coming from someone who isn't a team player or who doesn't understand the business value of time-to-market. Organizational business units reinforce an insular view: just focus on your own product, keep your head down, and let's get through the next quarterly profits call.

But when a digital product is part of a single company's portfolio of software, like the apps on your phone or the various pieces of Google's massive infrastructure, the importance of product management by design becomes obvious, for a simple reason. People's goals naturally intersect with a number of products in the portfolio, and a "siloed" approach to product management that may be organizationally easy to maintain begins to make life for your users really, really hard.

For example, Google's e-mail product, Gmail, could be thought of as a stand-alone silo of a product. It has a finite and manageable number of features, and it can be built by a finite and manageable number of developers. Not only that, but the team can be incentivized based on goals that are local to the product, and can even track profit and loss at a local business unit level.

But the people who *use* Gmail don't use it in a silo, and they don't consider e-mail as a stand-alone activity distinct from managing their contacts, getting mapping directions, or booking meetings. Most people don't think of Gmail as a product at all. They consider, instead, that they need to perform an action to achieve a goal, such as "I need to chat with you about something important but I'm afraid you'll freak out, so I want to do it in a public space and I want us to meet at a coffee shop." Or, "I need to find out when everyone is available to have a conference call, because conference calls are so fun and awesome."

In these cases, part of achieving the goal is about sending an e-mail. Another part is about looking at a calendar. Another part is about finding the address of a coffee shop, and still another is about finding driving directions to that location. These activities stretch *across* products. The arbitrary confines of Google's organizational structure should have little bearing on a person's ability to achieve his goal with ease. *Product management by design* implies a broad philosophy that champions for users in all aspects of building a product. This frequently means doing things that are organizationally hard, like getting Google's maps team to talk to its mail team. This may mean driving organizational alignment *in spite of conflicting incentive structures or revenue reporting models.*

There are other unique qualities of *product management by design*. Designers frequently take an optimistic view of the future, hold a skeptical view of technology for technology's sake, and utilize a process that's simultaneously iterative, divergent, and integrative. Designers learn to trust their informed intuition and to move forward with incomplete data, to accept the risks implicit in driving innovation, and to use visual artifacts as their primary mechanism for communication.

While they probably won't help you decorate your house, designers like things to look great, too.

THINKING VISUALLY, CREATIVELY, OPTIMISTICALLY, AND INTUITIVELY

Design is about humanizing technology or finding ways for technology to integrate into the fabric of our culture. Early designers worked to *hide* technology by wrapping the innards of consumer electronics in plastic casing. But the ubiquity of technological progress has introduced digitization in everything from cans of soup to air travel, so hiding technology is no longer a realistic goal. In many ways, technology hides on its own, because it's so prevalent.

Today's designers work to make technology *fit appropriately into our human-to-human interactions*. When you bring design to product management, you'll find that your natural tendency is to be skeptical of technological advancement as an end in itself, skeptical of cool for cool's sake. Instead, you must perceive technology as a means toward a larger end, and that larger end is to help people achieve their goals and realize their hopes and dreams.

The design process is visual and uses visual artifacts to communicate process, ideas, and solutions. Visual thinking is a way to play with ideas and to refine them. Designers use whiteboards, sketches, comics, and diagrams to communicate their thoughts. This visualization acts as a way to try ideas, to explore the multiple trajectories at once, to view the way things *might be*, and to craft the optimistic narratives of the future in a way that are accessible to everyone else. When you bring design to product management, visual thinking becomes the way in which you'll bring ideas to life.

Design takes an optimistic stance about the future by assuming that there are infinite ways to work to improve situations. Rather than attempting to reduce a situation to one best or optimized solution, designers seek to explore the situation space, to see multiple potentials for improvement, and to always consider *what might be*. One way of characterizing this approach is integrative thinking.

Roger Martin, dean of the Rotman School of Management at the University of Toronto, explains that this way of thinking is common across industry leaders: "Over the past six years, I have interviewed more than 50 such leaders, some for as long as eight hours, and found that most of them share a somewhat unusual trait: They have the predisposition and the capacity to hold in their heads two opposing ideas at once. And then, without panicking or simply settling for one alternative or the other, they're able to creatively resolve the tension between those two ideas by generating a new one that contains elements of the others but is superior to both."[1] When you bring design to product management, you'll find you've enhanced your ability to live in between ideas, and you'll increasingly be able to introduce this integrative thinking into your work.

Because designers conceive of what does not yet exist, their process cannot be analytically proven until after the fact. That means that they must make intuitive or inferential leaps. This plays out, tactically, as a form of interpretation, translating amorphous wants and needs into a tangible solution. Designers learn to move forward with just enough data, but even the most informed intuitive leap will occasionally be wrong. While they may work to minimize inferential errors, the design process is one that must accept innovation risk. Innovation risk is the chance that a new product, system, or service may fail. The larger the risk, the larger the reward. Similarly, the larger the innovation risk, the deeper the repercussions of failure.

After eighteen months of expensive development, Apple's Power Mac G4 was launched in 2000 with an iconic—*designed*—square shape and at a considerable manufacturing cost.[2] Apple discontinued it in just a year,

after selling only 150,000 units.[3] Steve Jobs explained the failure as a lack of audience: "The disappointment to us was the market wasn't as big as we thought."[4]

Lack of audience is a product management failure. The responsibility for understanding the potential market for an innovation falls squarely on the shoulders of the product manager. Jobs couldn't *know* people wouldn't buy the product until after launching it. As a product manager—and an innovator—he accepted the risk of the innovation, prepared to reap the benefits of success, and was aware of the likelihood of failure. When you bring design to product management, you'll find yourself taking on larger risks and being more confident in trusting your intuition, because your intuition will be shaped by empathy with the people that you hope to help and empower. You won't eliminate failure, but because you'll be taking bigger leaps, your successes will be larger and more obvious.

BRINGING DESIGN THINKING TO PRODUCT MANAGEMENT

One school of thought in product management, called "lean," prescribes the development of a "minimum viable product" (MVP), urging teams to create something, anything, as quickly as possible and get it into the hands of real people in order to test it, measure the results, and make small improvements. This, it is claimed, forces a scientific approach to product development: rhetoric, vision, and strategy are subjective, but use is objective and can be measured. Once a product has been launched, the team can then analyze usage patterns, iterate based on that usage, and drive an objective process with little chance of failure.

While this scientific process may successfully drive incremental product enhancements, it does little for producing leapfrog-style innovations. When you leverage a design process, you'll be pursuing a decidedly different approach, one that may be fundamentally at odds with the scientific measurement

ideas of lean product development. MVP and lean methodologies purport to be fast. Design is slow and not just because it takes longer. Because it's reflective, contemplative, and methodical, design encourages marinating and stewing, exploring and dreaming. These aren't *efficient* qualities—design doesn't claim to be efficient—but the process described in this book is rigorous, methodical, and highly regimented. (See table 1-1.)

This process is also highly cultural, personal, and emotional. It *celebrates* bias, one that's extraordinarily dependent on your *having a point of view*. It is not analytical or empirical, and if you approach it from an analytical perspective and attempt to tame it with measurement, you will be disappointed.

Table 1-1

Product development process transitions

MOVING FROM A TRADITIONAL PRODUCT DEVELOPMENT PROCESS:	TO A LOOSE AND LEAN PROCESS:	TO A DESIGN PROCESS:
Focuses on what the market seems to need	Focuses on what people say	Focuses on what people do
Attempts to minimize bias (and risk) by removing outliers and regressing to an "average" perspective	Attempts to minimize bias (and risk) by testing as frequently as possible	Embraces outliers and the implicit risk associated with celebrating eccentricities
Celebrates technological advancement and features as ends in themselves	Views technological advancement positively as a medium for rapid ideation and testing	Views technology advancement skeptically, as a means to an end but not as a goal
Tends to be found in a highly analytical culture	Tends to be found in a highly analytical culture	Tends to be found in a highly visual culture
Attempts to predict market behavior	Attempts to test market behavior	Attempts to provoke market behavior
Defines value in terms of utility—what a new product or service can do	Defines value in terms of utility—what a new product or service can do	Defines value in terms of emotion—how a new product or service makes someone feel

Design is extraordinarily effective—as a research process; in understanding and empathizing with what people want, need, and desire; and as a production process in creating beautiful, highly usable artifacts, systems, and services. I've taught the skills and methods presented in this book to executives at major *Fortune* 500 corporations; to consultants at product, military, and government entities; and to students who are just starting out. They are all surprised to learn how natural the process feels and equally surprised to see how powerful it is in shaping innovative and compelling products.

I show the techniques and process I describe in this book applied primarily to digital products, but the methods work with nondigital products, too. In fact, you can use these methods in the context of services, organizational structures, policy challenges, and anywhere else where human beings are dealing with the complexity of societal and technological changes. A colleague of mine has used these techniques to help the military find alternative approaches to dealing with sexual abuse in its ranks. Another colleague recently used this process with Unicef to help drive "Last Mile" health-care delivery in rural areas.

When I was writing this book, my editor at Harvard Business Review Press told me that "I also came to an interesting realization as I read through the manuscript—I *am* a product manager and have been for a long time, as a book acquisitions editor. I try to recognize potential market and personal, emotional, and intellectual impact in prospective book projects. I endeavor to get my team excited about the vision for the book in signing it up. I partner with authors in developing the 'product.' Our team partners with authors in thinking carefully about the market for the book and how to reach it. We launch the 'product' and carefully watch the response of users." This process is broadly applicable across industries and cultures, and is increasingly necessary as more jobs require managing an ambiguous creative process.

When you bring design to product management, you will find out what people want, need, and desire, and then you will craft products that will help or delight them. This approach to product management is about finding spirit and soul, and when you introduce design into your process, you'll experience a new level of emotional resonance and a unique connection with the people who use your product.

- -

AN INTERVIEW WITH JOE GEBBIA,
ON CREATIVE ROLES AND INTUITION

- -

Joe Gebbia is chief product designer at Airbnb, where he defines the Airbnb experience. He is dedicated to creating an inspiring and effortless user experience through sharp, intuitive design, and crafts the product road map to make it so. Gebbia values products that simplify life and have a positive impact on the environment and ensures that the company adheres to these tenets.

- -

JOE, HOW DOES A PAINTER END UP RUNNING ONE OF THE HOTTEST START-UPS OF THE YEAR?

I went to art school, and when I got there, I discovered that there's this thing called industrial design. It never before occurred to me that the objects in our lives have all been designed by somebody. I became very intrigued and said to myself, "I would much rather apply creativity to solving problems and improving people's lives than improving the state of the art world." I shifted gears away from painting, and during the course of learning industrial design, I started to understand some of the best practices and best approaches for designing things that truly solve problems for people. I'm reminded of a quote from the former president of the Rhode Island School of Design (RISD), John

Maeda: "Art raises questions, design answers questions." I've always been innately interested in how creativity can be applied to improve someone's life.

My first project out of school was a consumer product—a seat cushion—called Critbuns. It was a cushion inspired by really uncomfortable design critiques back at school. It was a foam cushion, and you could sit on it during your critique. The whole purpose was to get an idea from my sketchbook to the shelf of a store. It was a real-world exercise, identifying the mysterious gap between sketchbook and store.

I figured that out, and Critbuns made it all the way to the MoMA store in New York City. It was my first company and taught me all sorts of lessons about product development. The best way to learn about product development, to learn the difference between design and product management, is to start something and do everything yourself. You'll intimately understand the tensions between the creative side and the "ship it" side. At some point, you have to converge, stop ideating, and get to the point where you can produce it, ship it, code it, and manufacture it. It was a wonderful lesson to see what was actually involved. I wasn't acting as a consultant, where my role would end and my work would get handed off. I wasn't working in a big organization, where I would be confined to a certain part of the process and someone else would pick it up and I would never see it again. The fastest way to understand what product is all about is to do it all yourself. That was a good lesson, early in my career.

There's an issue with industrial design that I call designer's guilt. You realize, at a certain point—and this happened to me pretty early on—that if you are designing stuff, that stuff gets manufactured. For me, there's this heavy guilt about designing things that would eventually contribute to a landfill, because with consumer products, everything has an end of life. After a day, a decade, a hundred years, eventually, the thing gets thrown away. That's a great conflict for a designer. You are learning to make stuff, and then all of the sudden you have this wake-up call. I started to wonder: what are ways that you can apply design to the world without creating more stuff?

That inspired a second start-up, which was about helping designers connect with sustainable materials online. This was in 2006, and it brought me to the internet world. Because of it, I realized the beauty of no stuff. By having a web service, there was no fulfillment, no manufacturing, no warehousing. The social mission of the company was to connect designers with sources of environmentally considered materials, like recycled plastics, reclaimed timber, or organic cotton. I got to see the product development and design process applied in the context of the internet, for the virtual world. There are some really great principles from industrial design that translate to the web, like usability and empathy. In order to understand who you are designing for, you have to step into their shoes. That was a lesson I learned at RISD. I worked on a medical design project in school, and in order to understand how to go about solving it, we talked to patients, and doctors, and nurses. We went to the hospital. There was a moment when we lay down in the hospital bed and had the device applied to us. We became the patient. That's a principle that's carried over from industrial design to the web, this idea of "becoming the patient." It doesn't matter what form your product takes; it can be physical, a service, or an app. The best way to empathize and truly solve someone's problem is to live it and feel it firsthand.

In the course of doing the second start-up, I ran out of money and had to figure out how to pay the rent. To make money, my roommate bought some air beds and rented them out for a conference. It turned out that we were on to a much bigger idea than just a weekend project. Now here we are with Airbnb. The arc of the story is that I started with a physical product, with manufacturing and shipping, and it was 100 percent atoms. The arc has transcended now to a place where not only is there nothing physical produced, but we're inspiring hundreds of thousands of hosts all over the world to repurpose the space they already have and to make it more efficient. We're replacing the inefficiencies that exist in the world, and we've unlocked this new economic model in the process. We've inspired other people to go out and apply the economic theory to other industries, or vertically, like cars or parking spots or event spaces or coworking spaces. It's been dubbed the "sharing economy."

I'm swimming in the middle of the perfect soup right now and it feels great. We're not making any stuff, and we've inspired not only the people who use our service to be more resourceful, but adjacent industries to think, "Wow, how could we apply those same principles and be more efficient with the resources we have?"

YOU'VE DISCUSSED DESIGN AND PRODUCT AS THOUGH THEY WERE TWO SEPARATE THINGS. ARE THEY SEPARATE FUNCTIONS AT AIRBNB?

In the early days of a company, when it's three guys in an apartment, you just *make*. There's not a lot of planning. You're just making. You have no time for a great deal of research. There's just making and shipping. You watch the numbers and see how people respond to what you made, and you iterate like crazy. It's easy to do that when you are really small.

But as your organization gets bigger, you have to work very hard to keep design and development close together. There's a natural inertia that wants to separate those two things. I visualize our organization at Airbnb as two concentric circles, and where they overlap in the middle—which is the majority of the real estate of the circles—is what we call the product team. The left circle is engineering, the right is design, and the overlap is product. We want to do the best that we can to delineate between an engineer and a designer and product management, but reinforce this notion that we're all on the same team. It doesn't matter what your discipline is, because we're building the same service together. At the end of the day, customers don't give a crap who worked on what, and what kind of engineer was involved, and so on. They don't care. They just want a great service. It's important to us to keep those circles as close together as possible. It influences how we lay out the office, how we structure our meetings, how we socialize with each other, and how we share information and insights. We try to cohabitate as much as we can, which is hard, because as teams evolve, they get more specialized. The more specialized you get, the further apart things become.

WHY HAVE A DELINEATION AT ALL?

Should an engineer be designing? Should a designer be writing code? There are schools of thought that say a designer should be able to code and be able to create what he works on. I don't believe in that school of thought. I like finding people who are insanely passionate, who can go laterally across several things, and super-deep into one specific thing. If a designer is learning how to code, he isn't designing. It's unclear to me how learning to code makes his design better in the long run. I would rather make a culture that is super-collaborative, where the specialists in design and the specialists in development can sit side by side and work on a project together, so they can each play to their strengths.

WHEN YOU HAD JUST A FEW PEOPLE, WITH NO REAL ORGANIZATIONAL ROLES DELINEATED, PRODUCT VISION WAS PROBABLY PRETTY EASY TO COMMUNICATE BECAUSE IT WAS SHARED. HOW DO YOU COMMUNICATE IT NOW, WITH A BIGGER TEAM AND A DIFFERENT ORGANIZATIONAL STRUCTURE?

The best way to communicate a product vision is through a story. At the beginning of the year, we did an exercise where I asked each member of the product team (engineers, designers, producers) to e-mail me their favorite customer testimonial from 2012. I asked them to send me their favorite story from a guest or host on Airbnb that they connected with the most. Then I asked them, "If you were to help contribute to building out our services here in an extraordinary way this year, what kind of e-mail will you get this December?" I asked them to write a fictitious future testimonial, a story that represents them doing the best coding or design that they've ever done. If they did the best work they've ever done, this would be the kind of e-mail they would get.

The team's aspirational stories were incredible. The team had such imagination and insight into what issues we are facing and were able to describe the direction of the product. We took all of those stories and bound them in a book and sent it back to the entire team. The book gave a lens into the types of things we could be creating together. I participated, too; my story was at the front, the very first one.

Two people have sent me e-mails they've gotten from customers that are eerily similar to what they wrote back in February. It's not word for word, but the messages were similar to what they had imagined. The approach to how a vision gets communicated from me to the product team is different, because it's an opportunity for everyone to express himself and be heard. They can describe *their* vision. Any organization has a balance of things that are top down and bottom up. I don't want to create a dictatorship, a command that comes down from the mountain. You have to dance this line between having a vision and being inclusive so people have ownership of that vision. This was an exercise into that.

WHEN YOU RECEIVED ALL OF THESE GREAT IDEAS, HOW DID YOU PRIORITIZE?

We hire really creative people on purpose and have no shortage of directions in which we could go. So we have a general principle of being "vision led, customer informed." As a company, we certainly have a vision of where the product is going. We generally have a North Star that we are all headed toward. But I couldn't tell each employee exactly how to get there, nor would I want to. I would rather hire really smart people to help us figure that out. A vision gets projected outward, but it's done in a way that points to opportunities rather than solutions. We talk about where we're headed by talking about the opportunity. We don't say that we'll launch this or that feature by next year, or that we expect it to have these bullet points. Instead, we articulate an experience that we want to create for people who use the service in the future. Then we look to the team to fill in the blanks.

IS THAT IDEALIZED EXPERIENCE DRIVEN MORE BY DATA OR BY YOUR COLLECTIVE INTUITION?

Data is important, and there's plenty of it around here. We log everything and have all of the big data you could hope for. We have an incredibly robust analytics team helping us discover things. That data can tell you what's happening on the site. It can tell you how many people clicked on something or didn't click, how many people finished a form or didn't finish it, or how many people moved through a flow. But data doesn't answer the question *why*. You may have designed this beautiful flow and gotten someone to list a space on the site, but he might drop out halfway through. The data can show that all day long. But the data doesn't say why that happened.

That's where the research and insights side comes into the picture. We go in, qualitatively, and talk to guests and hosts to help extract the *why*. We ask them to walk through a flow and tell us about what's happening. We try to understand at a human level, not a data level, what's going through people's minds, what their concerns are in the moment of use. We try to learn about the experiences they are hoping to have that we haven't fulfilled for them.

If you have a crazy new approach or idea for something, you can't measure it. I like this quote from George Lois, one of the first ad men, in *Esquire* magazine: "Great ideas can't be tested. Only mediocre ideas can be tested." It sums up how I feel about trying to measure radical ideas. You simply can't. You can't apply data to see if you should do a radical idea. You do the radical idea, and then you measure how it worked. If we made decisions purely based on numbers, we would have quit. The numbers for many months told us to quit, to work on something else, because this idea was not going to take off. We don't always make decisions based on numbers.

WHEN THE NUMBERS WERE TELLING YOU TO GIVE UP, HOW DID YOU KNOW TO IGNORE THEM AND TO TRUST YOUR GUT?

Because we had an experience that we could reflect on. The three air beds and three guests that we hosted sparked all this—we could draw on a real-world experience. We lived through a prototype, and we knew what it felt like. We were married to the problem. We understood it in a way that others didn't. We felt strongly that, if we stuck with it, others would see what we saw. People would find delight in sharing their space and meeting people they otherwise wouldn't have met. We had every reason to believe that if people just saw what we saw, and experienced what we experienced, they would be into it.

We have a classic story about this. In the many months that the business was failing, we took a risk. Hosts were putting up pictures of their apartments that were blurry or were taken at night, and were really not desirable places to stay. We said, let's go solve that problem. Let's fly to New York, where we had thirty listings, and take really nice pictures for hosts for free. No charge to them. So we went to New York, met some hosts, took some pictures of their apartments, and within a week, revenue doubled. When I say doubled, it went from $200 to $400. But that was huge! For months, it hadn't gone over $200. We were on the brink of folding the company. Thank goodness we left behind the notion that in the world of technology, you're supposed to do stuff in a scalable way.

We tried that, in the early days, and failed miserably. Scaling is the wrong approach when looking for product-market fit. You have no scale to solve for when you are starting something. So why optimize for that? When we decided to take the photos, we turned the company around. We actually started to understand, because those photos helped us interact with our hosts. They told us about all the problems they were having with the service. And we learned something. When we learned something, we iterated the service for them and they started using it more. That's why revenue doubled. We went back the next weekend and took more photos, and revenue doubled again. We did this for five weeks straight, and revenue doubled week over week. It's crazy when we look at the graph in retrospect.

That was the turning point. By doing something that didn't scale, we turned the company around. What's cool is that now we've taken the photography operation and scaled it out—we have a team here in San Francisco that manages three thousand contract photographers in every major city around the world. There's a really easy way to click and get professional photos for free. It doesn't cost a host anything.

JOE, IF YOU WERE TALKING TO SOMEONE WHO WANTED TO DO WHAT YOU'VE DONE—GET INTO PRODUCT AND BUILD A BUSINESS AROUND A HUMAN SERVICE— WHAT WOULD YOU TELL THEM?

I would tell them to build something. Right now, it's never been easier to make things. It's never been easier to create an app or a website. The resources out there are enormous, and the cost to access them has never been this low. I would encourage them to make stuff. Get your hands as dirty as possible. Throw yourself into an experience of making. Coding, or design, or whatever it is, learn it, and make something. It's not like there have to be 10 million people using it. It might be just your friends or yourself. But you made something, and you shipped it.

product-market fit
finding broad appeal

Joe has only been at LiveWell for two weeks, but at the moment, it feels more like two years. The leadership team members were serious when they said they were pivoting their business. They've essentially agreed to start from scratch, throwing away any go-to-market strategy that may have existed and killing thousands of lines of code that have already been written. True to their word, they've been looking to Joe to identify the process by which the new product will come to life. He's never felt more intimidated; he's also never felt more alive in his life.

He's been leading the group through a series of facilitation exercises aimed at understanding the health and wellness market in order to identify a space in which to develop a new product. The group has more or less lived in the war room, where now Joe absentmindedly nudges a pizza box off the table so he has more room to draw. He's sketching a market map of wearable devices, all of which claim to help people track their biometric data.

The conversations among the team members have converged on personal measurement as a potential opportunity space. This sounds great, but the team is skeptical of building a physical product. Can it avoid the capital expenditure of producing and selling hard goods and somehow leverage software as a solution?

Joe's broad goal is to understand the market well enough that he can carve out a space for the new product to live, a space that's full of opportunity but not overly crowded with competitors. His more specific goal is to gain just enough confidence in a direction so he can leave the building and go talk to real people. Joe is convinced that he only needs a few more pieces to the market story before he can develop a research plan. He's in an uncomfortable place, because he's trying to understand product-market fit, but he doesn't even have a product yet.

In chapter 1, we looked at how a design process champions for and focuses on people. One way to focus on people is in a general sense, as a community or population. In the context of consumer products, we could refer to this population as the *market* and describe Joe's goal as "ensuring *product-market fit*." This describes the relationship between a product and a vague idea of the "market." This complex idea simultaneously includes the various competitors, stakeholders, suppliers, and distributors of a product or service. It encapsulates economics, but in a practical rather than a theoretical sense; it describes financers, consumers, advertisers, and stores. If you can achieve product-market fit, your product will be financially successful. The terms to judge success are relative. A new product may achieve product-market fit simply by gaining visibility among early adopters, while an established product might need to turn massive profits or disrupt the competition in order to claim product-market fit.

You'll note that I've chosen the word "fit" on purpose instead of a word like "sales" or "performance." Profit and revenue are important, but the relationship between the product and the market is more complex than simply the number of units sold. This fit describes the way the market broadly responds to what you have to offer, including competitive positioning, collaborative relationships, and even technological adoption.

A market may not be ready for a certain product. While a product concept may seem quite valuable, society as a whole may lack the cultural and technological infrastructure to support that product. For example, global positioning systems (GPSs) existed as early as 1973, and individual consumer GPS units were sold as early as 2000, but most consumers didn't have a broad and simple conduit to use or understand this technology until Apple introduced maps in the iPhone in 2007.[1] Microwave technology was developed in the late 1930s and commercialized in the late 1940s, but didn't catch on until we had a cultural respect for the technology as a safe form of cooking—some fifty years later.[2] Historically this pattern repeats itself over and over. A technology will be developed and refined, but it lacks a cultural "container," so, unable to understand it, we ignore it.

This pattern can also happen in the reverse way. We can broadly understand a technology, but the technology may not be quite as ready for us as we are for it. Consider AT&T's U-verse product, a way to bring digital cable to the home. The product depends on a certain kind of fiber-optic cable being available to the home. Copper wiring, the more traditional way of bringing cable to a house, is broadly available; fiber-optic cable is less common. A customer out of range is out of luck. Even if that customer is willing to pay whatever AT&T wants to charge, she can't use the product until the critical path is shortened. This problem is often called the "last mile" problem: how can the company gain market traction without rolling out a massive capital-intensive infrastructure between each fiber node and the home, servicing the huge amount of last-mile connections?

U-verse and other cable providers have created a roundabout solution to this problem. They can bring their high-speed service to nodes that are within five thousand feet of customer homes using fiber and then use cheaper copper for the last mile, but the service is notably slower. If a handful of customers are provided poorer service, the company could easily choose to ignore them. However, if the actual go-to-market strategy requires broad-based rollout of this approach, the market will surely notice and complain. The product will have poor product-market fit until the delivery infrastructure is rolled out, which—as a capital-intensive investment is required to string fiber-optic cable to every home—might take years. Product-market fit is about the relationship between the product offering and *all* of the market constraints, including timing.[3]

WHAT IS "THE MARKET"?

To establish product-market fit, you'll need to understand the amorphous idea of "the market." The market is a space of customers, users, competitors, policies, laws, and trends. Say you've just developed a new application for the iPhone, and you are about to launch it into Apple's App Store. Your launch seems so simple: just upload the app. Think again, because you are about to engage:

- The community, made up of both people who pay for your product and those who don't. Some people may read about your product or use a trial version, or your application may be fully accessible for free. In all cases, nonpaying members of the community hold leverage over your reputation in their size and scale. Your product will have a community of users, even if you don't consider it a "social product," because the internet has established a social platform for conversation, debate, and training related to *any* product.

- Customers. The *community* is the top of the funnel—the maximum number of people who may *ever* use your product. *Customers*, on the other hand, are the people who have perceived enough value in your application to exchange money for it. Their expectations are high, even when the cost is low. In a world where digital applications are frequently provided for free, paying even a few dollars leads to expectations of quality, service, responsiveness, and most importantly, value. Customers need to realize the value that's been promised to them. Simplistically, the thing needs to work as advertised.

- Competitors, or companies that offer a similar product. They'll examine your product, consider the likelihood of you disrupting their market share, and act accordingly to ignore you, to appropriate your innovations, or worse—to eliminate your ability to deliver your product at all.

- Trends, or market tendencies that occur over time. Your product may be one of many small data points that converge to force a larger event, such as the creation of a new law or a competitive acquisition.

- Policies, or market-led artificial constraints on your product. Apple's App Store has a list of rules that determine your ability to offer product in its storefront. Some of these are predictable, like rules about obscenity or pornography. Others are both vague and surprising. For example, rule 2.12 states that "Apps that are not very useful or do not provide any lasting entertainment value may be rejected."[4] This provides Apple with a great deal of subjective policy control over your ability to bring a product to market.

- Laws, or government-led artificial constraints on your product. Your product may be against the law, or it may require specific evaluation and approval from a government agency. These constraints may limit your ability to respond to the market quickly, or they may completely defeat your ability to offer your product at all.

Achieving product-market fit means launching a product in a manner that gels with all of these facets. For example, consider how the facets of the market played out during the launch of Heyride, a ride-sharing application, in 2012 in Austin, Texas.

Heyride was started with the intent of disrupting the tired taxicab industry. Remember the last time you took a cab? Chances are pretty good that you felt that you paid too much to be driven at breakneck speed through the city by a grouchy driver in a cab that reeked of smoke, just to have him give you attitude about paying with a credit card at the end. Taxis sure seem ready for change, and Heyride wanted to provide that change. The company offered a simple mobile application so anyone could offer his or her car as a taxi. You could become a taxi driver by setting your price and your hours of availability, and accepting fares. Anyone could become a member of the *community* of drivers and riders. You could either volunteer to be a driver or you could download a companion application for free to explore car availability or to view reviews of drivers. If you flagged down a car using the application, you became a *customer*, and you could pay with your credit card.

Heyride is part of a larger *trend* toward collaborative consumption, the sharing economy, in which people utilize service offerings to share high-priced products, rather than purchasing them on their own.[5] For example, the popular short-term vacation rental site Airbnb allows people to share their houses with one another. NeighborGoods allows people to share their power tools with one another.

Some fields have become crowded with *competitors*, such as the shared automobile space. Companies like Car2Go, Zipcar, and Uber have various *policies* in place to mitigate increasing concerns from customers. For example, Uber recently shifted from using licensed limousine services to a model comparable to Heyride and, in doing so, added a number of policy-based safeguards like a $2 million insurance policy and background checks on all drivers.[6]

But for Heyride, *laws* stopped the company in mid-step. It was served a cease and desist letter from the City of Austin on October 31, 2012, arguing that it was violating various city regulations applicable to taxis. The response from Heyride's CEO was dismissive, as he publicly offered the statement that "I don't know how they'd enforce it . . . To me, that sounds like they're trying to strike fear into the heart of people who are giving rides to each other."[7] Not three months later, Heyride was acquired by SideCar, another ride-sharing company. As of this writing, SideCar still has been unable to offer service in Austin.[8]

When I talked to Brian Romanko, formerly the chief technology officer of Heyride, he described the relationship between communities of passionate users and legislation change: "Policies are generally enacted with the public's best intentions in mind. However, lawmakers cannot predict the future. Heyride was only possible because of new technologies, such as GPS-enabled smartphones, and changing consumer opinions toward ownership as evidenced by growth of the sharing economy. These were not considerations when legislators wrote the transportation policies. Unfortunately, these policies also become protective shields around incumbent players. Never underestimate the lengths to which existing constituents will go to protect themselves from disruption."

For Heyride, SideCar, and all of the other companies in this space, *the market* is undergoing massive fluctuation. The rate of technological adoption of mobile phones has blown past the rate of local legislation, and each day brings new innovations in regulated industries. The City of Austin's response to Heyride is a likely example of how other cities will respond as these services seek to expand. As municipalities catch up, product owners are forced to interact with new market constituents, rules, and regulations. They must track precedent set in other cities, while simultaneously pushing their own disruptive innovations forward.

Romanko's advice for founders in these situations is to focus on user growth—growing passionate advocates—rather than directly on policy change: "If a product runs counter to current public policy, the best path to success is building a strong base of consumer support. Elected officials are representatives. They have an obligation to consider policy changes. The more passionate users you have supporting your disruption (and proving, through repeated use, that the existing policies are overreaching or ill-conceived), the greater your chances of changing the status quo."

The market ecosystem is so complicated. To think with clarity about product-market fit and to help a product survive, it's necessary to actively track signals in the market.

SEEKING SIGNALS FROM THE MARKET

A signal is a clue, a small piece of data; on its own, a signal is ineffective. But in a group, and with thoughtful interpretation, signals act as a driving force for your market strategy. The story of Heyride is ripe with signals. A quote in its press release can be a signal, such as announcing a new relationship with politicians or describing new market positioning. The user-interface decisions in its product are signals, indicating how its product may shift in the future. The blog post from a competitive product owner can act as a signal, illustrating its competitive intent or the way it thinks about the market.

Interpreting signals requires time and experience, and because it's subjective, it adds risk. A signal is objective and neutral; an interpretation is biased. This interpretative risk can both position your product for success or doom it to failure. No pressure. Your first job in understanding product-market fit is establishing a cadence in gathering and systematically interpreting signals, and selecting just the signals that can help you build insights around a product vision, while shrugging off signals that can overwhelm you or leave you paralyzed with inaction.

IGNORING SIGNALS FROM THE COMPETITION

You might be tempted to consider the functionality of a competitor's product as a benchmark and treat its product as your primary source of signals. After all, its product offers a very straightforward message of how a company views its market opportunity. Competitive analysis is a common method used to track what the competition has already done or how it has already positioned itself. Yet competitive analysis is misleading if it is positioned as a guide for product development, because it encourages the bunch-and-swarm mentality: "Because the competition built these features, we too must build these features to remain at parity." Knowing the features in a competitor's product is interesting. Copying them is not, and there are three reasons why:

I. First, the development of features takes time and resources, and development efforts are zero-sum games. If you attempt to build everything the competition is doing, you won't be building things the competition *isn't* doing. You will find yourself fighting simply to keep up. This is precisely the situation both Microsoft and Netscape found themselves in during the browser wars of the late nineties. As one company released a new version of its product, the other company rushed to copy each feature and embellish it a little to stand out from the other. There was no real consideration of what people needed or wanted. Instead, each company was myopically focused on what the other was doing. This is the product version of the pricing "race to the bottom" that consumer electronics companies often find themselves in, where their only method of differentiation is to cut their price below the competition. At least in the pricing game, consumers benefit from lower costs. In the product feature race to the bottom, everyone loses.

2. Next, the added complexity of extra features in a product *always* serves to diminish the experience a person will have with *any* features in that product. Quantifying and cataloging features for some internal organizational purpose may seem useful, but thinking about features usually comes at the expense of thinking about goals. There's even a way of computing the overhead of this complexity. Hick's Law describes the time it takes for a person to make a decision as a result of the possible choices he or she has in a product. Not surprisingly, Hick's Law is logarithmic: adding more features exponentially increases the amount of time a user takes to make a decision.

3. Finally, and most importantly, your product—and your competitors' products—should have a sense of character that's uniquely defined by the company's values and culture. The way company culture shapes a product is considerable (think about the way a Microsoft product *feels* versus the way an Apple product *feels*) and is largely irreproducible because the specific people who make a product can't be copied. Noting and taking the market leader's

features doesn't get you its employees, its working environment, or its work ethic, and most importantly, it doesn't get you the same emotional resonance. It would be fairly simple to create an online shoe store that matches the functionality and inventory of Zappos, but it would be really, really hard to match the customer service and trust for which the company is known. Would you, for example, chat casually on the phone with a customer for ten hours to describe what it's like to live in Las Vegas—which is exactly what happened to a Zappos customer loyalty team member? The employee wasn't reprimanded for being off topic or for wasting time, because he was doing his job, engaging in whatever conversation the customer wanted to have. For Zappos, inventory of shoes is important, but the character of the company is *more* important.[9]

You might also be tempted to absorb signals from competitors about their market behavior, such as their acquisitions or their external marketing. These signals build daily. You'll watch trends in product launches, you'll observe market movement, and you will even become aware of *talent* movement. When Yahoo hired Marissa Mayer from Google, it sent signals to product managers at companies engaged in mail, search, advertising, maps, and any of the hundreds of other areas of Yahoo's business. These signals aren't interpreted in isolation. A product manager starts to integrate these signals into a worldview of the market, a frame of reference for her own product and her own career. A product manager at Facebook would interpret the hiring of Mayer quite differently than a product manager at Twitter, but you can bet both noticed it and spent time reflecting on how this might change the competitive landscape for their respective products.

These signals are noise and are largely a distraction from your core task. Rather than focusing on what the competition says and does, consider that product data about *the market* can be gathered more successfully from two other places: the way a *community responds to the competition*, and the way in which *the competition engages with technological advancement*.

EMBRACING SIGNALS FROM THE COMMUNITY

Perhaps the richest source of market signals comes from watching a community of people, for these people—by definition—share norms and have values in common. The signals that are most exciting within the group are shifts in attitudes, changes in rules, and the challenging of conventions, for these shifts indicate changes in values. When you start to sense this type of shift becoming a pattern, you've stumbled on something really, really valuable.

Consider the community of young, liberal voters that came together to vote, for the first time, in President Obama's first election. Over a period of twelve months prior to the election, a visible change in attitude could be observed as a generation of generally apolitical youth became increasingly engaged and vocal in politics for the first time. This is a *culture shift*, evidenced as a *community shift*. People who shared various qualities (such as age or socioeconomic status) began to share *values,* too. To those outside the community—to older generations or younger voters who weren't interested in Obama's politics—the shift is downright confusing and appears to come out of nowhere, driven by invisible forces. Yet for those *inside* the community, the shift feels like a natural evolution of their thinking, as their frame of reference evolves and is reinforced by group behavior.

You can observe this same type of value shift occur within broad online communities like Reddit or within niche-based online communities like FlyerTalk or MetaFilter. When Yahoo announced the acquisition of Tumblr, a portion of the Tumblr community reacted negatively, with seventy-two thousand blogs switching to the blogging platform WordPress in an hour.[10] To be aware of this shift and to understand the relevance of it, you'd need to actively engage with that community. Is seventy-two thousand people a lot? Is this a fringe feeling, or is it representative of the entire population of users? What's the prevalent frame, the tone of discourse, and what are the norms and mores embraced by the community? If you immerse yourself in the community, over time you'll be able to discern when these things start to *change*. It is the *change* in frame, tone, or norms that offers you product insight. These are the most useful signals you can gather from the market as broad indicators of value changes. The acquisition of Tumblr by Yahoo signals growth for its venture capitalists, a change in strategy for Yahoo, and a large amount of money changing hands. None of these signals are nearly as interesting for *your* product as the signal of its community potentially abandoning its platform of expression.

In 2007, someone wrote code that cracked the digital rights management on a popular media format called HD DVD. The code was posted as an article to the online community Digg. Over ten thousand people gave the article the thumbs-up, and it grew in popularity. But the site, fearing legal repercussion from big media companies, responded with a heavy hand. It removed the article, banned the person who posted it, and continued to restrict communication on the topic. The community members revolted, because the topic meant a lot to them. Eventually, the revolt grew so strong that founder Kevin Rose responded to the controversy: "But now, after seeing hundreds of stories and reading thousands of comments, you've made it clear. You'd rather see Digg go down fighting than bow down to a bigger company. We hear you, and effective immediately we won't delete stories or comments containing the code and will deal with whatever the consequences might be."[11] This type of signal is pivotal to shaping product decisions: being aware of how a community shift like this happens will help you better drive the philosophy of your own products. To be aware of the community shift, you'll need to be a part of the community.

ABSORBING PATTERNS OF TECHNOLOGICAL ADVANCEMENT AND DESIGN

Design can help humanize technology, and the process is easier if the people in your target market believe a given technology will help them. Studying market signals can highlight how common or broad this change in attitude has become.

From a broad, conceptual perspective, consider that it was first thought strange, and then rude, to hold a conversation via a Bluetooth headset while in public. Now it's considered normal to see someone talking to himself with a small device in his ear. Answering phone calls in public places like buses, airports, and restaurants has, unfortunately, become commonplace. This indicates both a cultural acceptance of wearable technology and an increasing familiarity with the speaker "being private in public." Both of these shifts help simplify the introduction of more pronounced (and visibly strange) innovations like Google Glass or other wearable camera technologies, because they both point to a design pattern for advanced technology: that public use of a wearable computer to conduct traditionally private activities is socially acceptable.

For an example that's more established, consider the introduction of the computer mouse—a device that most of us would consider as obvious as a table or chair. Yet the interface pattern is culturally bizarre; there's nothing natural or obvious about pushing a physical controller on your desk in order to control a digital tracking spot on a screen. Apple seemingly popularized the mouse overnight in the mid-1980s, and now other companies have built on top of this model. The basic paradigm of a graphic user interface blends into the background.

Both the mouse and Google Glass show how technology is integrated into our culture, and both examples show how you can productize technology that's existed for decades. If you are paying attention, you can catch signals of this process as it is happening. It works like this.

Major research labs at universities and public companies constantly drive new, exciting, and novel inventions, publishing them in little-known journals and presenting them at academic conferences. Often, this publication is a requirement for the funding that supports the research. In retrospect, these publications provide a historical trail for nearly every single innovation we enjoy in modern-day life. You can find the research that led to the mouse and wearable cameras in old archives of various engineering and computer journals, many of which are available for you to read for free online. You can watch a video of Doug Engelbart demonstrating the computer mouse in 1968, or view photos of Steve Mann wearing early models of Google Glass from 1981.[12] There's an obvious trail from research lab to commercial product, and then from commercial product to cultural backdrop.

However, to catch the trail, you need to be actively looking for it. Bill Buxton, a futurist at Microsoft, describes this as technological research that's "not *generally* known, but it's known to anyone who ducks their head below their radar to find it." He continues, "Anything that will be a billion dollar industry in 10 years is already 10 years old. If you study history, almost no one invented anything."[13] This slow process of technological humanization is a signal, but to catch the signal, you have to read those tech journals and attend those highly esoteric tech conferences.

These product innovations didn't happen overnight, and neither will flexible displays, collaborative touch screens, 3D printing of working electronics, or the host of other technologies that have already been publicly unveiled by researchers. Only when these technologies become affordable and—most importantly—humanized do they become visible in the products we know, use, and laud. The trick for you, as a product manager, is to become conversationally aware of these technological advancements so you can track their relative proximity to this point of humanization. These signals show up in technology journals that you've likely never heard of and in the proceedings from very specific conferences. In these publications you can find technology signals worth pursuing. By the time the popular media discovers the advancement, the signal has already been appropriated.

FRAMEWORKS TO SYNTHESIZE PRODUCT-MARKET SIGNALS

It's 11 p.m., and the team has made a great deal of progress. Everyone has gone home, but Joe's mind is running too fast for him to quit yet. He leans back in his chair and surveys the workspace. It looks like a productive, albeit messy, day.

The team has been sketching on the whiteboard and has developed a series of frameworks intended to place broad constraints around a product direction. It's been both rewarding and highly confusing, because the conversation has been simultaneously broad and specific. There's a list of two hundred product opportunities on one whiteboard, while another has a sketch of the market as a 2x2 matrix. The team has narrowed in on a software-based tool that helps people gain visibility into their health and wellness, and there's alignment around the vision. Joe experienced a quiet feeling of pleasure when the chief technology officer had scrawled, "Help people understand their own health and wellness," in giant letters at the top of the whiteboard.

This implicit vision statement has helped the team members identify a number of possible design ideas. Joe has been playing the role of police officer, making sure they don't actually pick any one of the ideas. It's been hard. His goal has been to develop a feeling for a market space, a trajectory in which they can move and explore, without actually committing to a specific set of functionality.

Joe feels good. He's achieved his goal. The team has developed a sense of alignment around a shared purpose, and the various artifacts on the wall serve to cement a conceptual area for exploration.

In chapter 1, we focused on absorbing signals from the market in order to drive product-market fit. But don't expect those signals to tell you what to build; that would be much too easy. The research you conduct is not definitive, nor is it predictive of success. Instead, market signals give you provocations. As you explore the market and observe community, technology, and product signals, you can start to develop *thinking artifacts* that help to interpret these provocations. The broad purpose of generating these artifacts is for you to gain knowledge, inform your insight, and help you establish a strategy and plan. The artifacts act as sieves through which you pour the signals. Some diagrams are *presentation artifacts*, used to rationalize your ideas to other people. Think of these, instead, as *working artifacts*. The purpose in creating them is to help you consider and establish strategy. Counterintuitively, once the artifacts have been made, they lose their value because they've already accomplished their goal: of informing your broad trajectory.

DEVELOPING A VALUE-GOAL STATEMENT

While you may be in charge of a *product*, shifting your thinking to *being in charge of value* is useful. When you synthesize the signals you find in the market, you can start to identify the value that you hope to deliver with your own product. This value speaks to human characteristics, like love, connection, respect, or pride. This value—not features—will differentiate you in the market, so it's useful to frame your value in terms of a market leader. (See table 2-1.)

The last entry in table 2-1 is a joke, but only kind of. When you shift from focusing on "the product" to "the value we strive to offer people,"

Table 2-1

How to frame your value

INSTEAD OF THINKING OF YOURSELF LIKE THIS . . .	TRY THINKING OF YOUR ROLE LIKE THIS . . .
I'm the product manager for Google Maps.	I help people gain confidence in finding their way quickly and effectively. Unlike Bing Maps, our product tries to anticipate what you'll search for based on your Google+ profile.
I'm the product manager for Airbnb.	I help people get a good night's sleep as they gain unique cultural experiences in a new city. Unlike a Hyatt hotel, our product introduces you to unique culture, lifestyle, and new friends.
I'm the product manager for United Airlines.	I make people physically and emotionally uncomfortable for long periods of time. Unlike Virgin Atlantic, our product forces people to conform to arcane policies and procedures.

your tendency to fall back on a tired brand promise is quickly placed in check. Put another way, it's difficult to hide behind a marketing message or slogan when you focus on value.

Clearly, these types of exercises can become politically charged. You may begin identifying aspirational qualities of your brand that conflict with company guidelines established by someone higher up the food chain than yourself. These may have been made with the best of intent, but with a very nonhuman focus. United Airlines' notoriously poor service is most likely due to a very purposeful set of cost-cutting measures made in an attempt to appease shareholders.[14] A value-goal statement for an airline like Virgin might read something like this: "I help travelers build memories in foreign lands by providing long-haul flights that are highly comfortable. Unlike United Airlines, our product frames a unique cultural experience on the ground with a soothing cultural experience in the air."

Airline differentiation doesn't come through the addition of engineering features, as these are largely table stakes. The plane needs to fly. The seats need to hold the weight of the passengers. Instead, differentiation will come by recognizing and catering toward the emotional and the experiential: how does it feel before, during, and after the flight? By writing a value-goal statement in the context of a market leader, and attempting to take an honest approach to your existing brand values, you can start to identify key emotional facets that can help you drive product differentiation.

DESCRIBING THE COMMUNITY WITH A 2X2 MATRIX

The value-goal statement identifies the type of value you aspire to provide and helps you make sense of the signals you've gathered. A 2x2 matrix is another way of making sense of those signals. It's a simple diagramming technique that frames a data set from two perspectives in order to understand the relationships latent in those two perspectives. You can use a 2x2 to synthesize and understand your product-market signals and to understand the communities that exist in the space you are exploring.

First, list the various community segments you've identified in your research—the different types of people who make up the community of potential users. During its brainstorming, Joe's team identified sixteen communities in the health and wellness space (see table 2-2).

Next, consider the various attributes of these communities that help define and differentiate them from one another. List both the factual attributes and also the emotional attributes.

Joe might start by asking himself, "What differentiates daily exercisers from the recently retired?" His answers might be, "The recently retired have a lot more time," or "Daily exercisers are younger," or "The recently retired have more anxiety about money." As he works through the various groups, he'll arrive at a list of attributes that describe the communities (see table 2-3).

Now, sketch a blank 2x2 diagram. Pick one factual or emotional attribute for the x-axis, and another for the y-axis. Start to put the communities on the diagram. You are trying to approximate their location

Table 2-2

Sixteen communities in the health and wellness space

Endurance triathletes (Ironman)	Yoga students	Cancer survivors	Vegans
Endurance runners (marathon)	Pilates students	Herbalists	Paleo dieters
Daily exercisers (i.e., Gold's Gym)	Bodybuilders	Children (team sports)	Weekend club athletes (adult team sports)
Underground fitness (i.e., CrossFit)	The recently retired	Women, post-pregnancy	Gluten-free dieters

Table 2-3

Attributes describing the sixteen communities in the health and wellness space

FACTUAL ATTRIBUTES	EMOTIONAL ATTRIBUTES
Quantity of population	Social stigma of joining
Cost necessary to participate	Perceived ease of joining
Equipment necessary to participate	Accompanied by introspection
Time commitment necessary to participate	Accompanied by anxiety
Physical availability	Fear of financial commitment
Age	Body-image issues

Figure 2-1

A 2x2 diagram for the health and wellness space

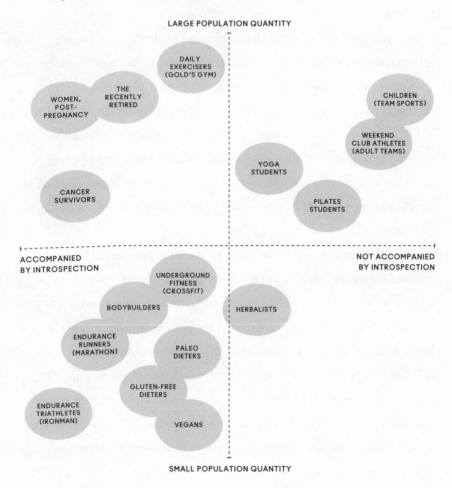

iterations on a given product tend to optimize code to be more efficient, and that optimization is an exercise in elimination. Refactoring is about increasing efficiency and simplicity, and reducing complexity.

Design, however, is frequently a generative activity. Designers consider multiple futures, thinking about different ways that the world *might* be.

relative to one another. If you don't know where they go, you'll need to conduct research to better understand them. We'll talk about how to do that research in the next chapter.

For example, Joe selected the attributes "quantity of population" and "accompanied by introspection"; the 2x2 that resulted is shown in figure 2-1.

You can see how Joe approximated the positioning of each community segment in order to show how it relates to those attributes. In Joe's diagram, there's white space in the top-left quadrant and the bottom-right quadrant. These gaps might indicate market opportunities, places for him to aim his product. Or, they might indicate areas where there is no market upside, places where he should avoid positioning his product.

Sketch another 2x2. Continue to explore the space, comparing attributes, and see what happens. Your goal is not to blaze through all of the combinations as quickly as possible, and the diagrams don't give you any definitive answers. Instead, your goal is to gain a sense of the space, to build a feeling about how the various communities intersect with one another, and to live in a playful head space of exploration. These diagrams are thinking tools to help you analyze a potential innovation from the various perspectives of the people who will benefit from it. Have conversations about the diagrams and try to define what each might mean to you and to your company.

PLAYING "WHAT IF?"

A philosophical way of thinking about engineering is as a reductive activity, in that an engineer *eliminates uncertainty* and *reduces potential outcomes* in order to identify and ultimately optimize for a single outcome. As a software developer writes a function, she commits to a strategy and a series of steps, and in doing so she eliminates other strategies or steps. Further development

This means examining and considering variations of ideas, allowing ideas to build on one another, and generating more, rather than reducing to less. Particularly at an innovation stage, the main question a designer asks and answers is, "What if?"

An industrial designer working on the form of a new coffeemaker might sketch hundreds or even thousands of slight variations in order to explore the form. Each sketch is provocative, in that it prompts the designer to think of new possibilities. While the question "What if?" is typically asked about products, it can be asked about market strategy, too. A sketch of a market strategy will prompt introspection, and this introspection can be visualized in alternative sketches. The results of sketching market strategy typically take the form of future scenarios of market movement.

Imagine that you are working at the small start-up Heyride, mentioned earlier, and focused on disrupting traditional taxi services by offering a collaborative car-sharing program. Your product is in development, and your initial product offering will be out in a few months. While you've already committed to product decisions, which are under your control, there are a host of market decisions that are out of your control. You can use what-if provocations to think about what product actions a competitor might take, and use these to your advantage:

- What if Yellow Cab releases a similar app in a similar time frame?
- What if a user of our product encounters a dangerous situation as a result of our product?
- What if users don't trust our product offering?
- What if we receive a negative review in the press?
- What if the city government doesn't recognize the legitimacy of our business and introduces legal challenges?

By asking what-if questions, you can provoke a fictional narrative of the future. You can imagine new scenarios and begin to plan on a course of action. Some of these questions may lead you to actions that mitigate risk. Others may introduce, change, or eliminate marketing activities. Still others may change the features of the product itself. Envisioning what your competitors might do in the future is different from looking at what they've already done. What-if thinking allows you to act strategically and preemptively, rather than simply respond in a feature-for-feature style.

IMAGINING LOSING

On the path toward developing product innovation, you might be tempted to look at a competitor's existing products and offerings, but the minute you do that you are already behind. The competitor's product already exists, and you can only react. You can get ahead, however, by presuming that a competitor will introduce a *new* product into the market. In this scenario, imagine that your product loses miserably to that new product. You can envision how the competitive offering is presented to the market, and as a result you'll be able to develop a likely competitive go-to-market strategy.

Start by considering your product sitting on a shelf in a store. (Remember when software was sold in boxes in stores? If it helps you imagine, you can pretend the store is called the App Store, and it's shaped like a giant iPhone.) Now, imagine a new competitive product sitting right next to it, and here come two shoppers strolling down the aisle. Both shoppers match your target audience, and they're talking loudly about what they intend to purchase. What conversation can you overhear when they approach the product category? How do they analyze and compare the two product offerings on the shelf? What are the compelling factors that attract them to one or the other, and how does their dialogue reflect their decision-making abilities?

As a strategic exercise, assume the shoppers purchase the competitive product. Why did they pick it? Was it the product messaging? The features and functions? Pricing? The brand reputation of the alternative company? The aesthetic of the packaging? Tell a story of a future in which your product loses. Why does it lose?

At this stage, it's useful to literally sketch the differentiator on a piece of paper. If the competitive product has a superior pricing strategy, sketch out how the product and capabilities are priced. If there's a unique functionality in the product, draw wireframes of how it will manifest itself. If the fake company has a superior organizational structure, draw it and identify what makes it better than yours. Write the press release announcing the competitive product release, and then write a fake *Wired* article of how your product—on superior market footing—was overwhelmed by that new entrant. Identify the weakness in your strategy that allowed the competitor to succeed when you, hypothetically, failed.

When you're done, you'll have the scaffold for a defensive product strategy.

AN INTERVIEW WITH JOSH ELMAN,
ON THE PROCESS OF PRODUCT MANAGEMENT

Josh Elman joined Greylock Partners, a venture capital firm, as a principal in 2011. Over the past fifteen years, Elman has worked in product and engineering roles at some of the leading companies in social, commerce, and media. Prior to Greylock, Elman was a product lead for growth and relevance at Twitter, and helped Twitter grow its active user base by nearly ten times. Before Twitter, he worked on the platform at Facebook and led the launch of Facebook Connect. Earlier in his career, Elman led product management for Zazzle, was part of the early team at LinkedIn focused on growth and jobs, and led product and engineering for RealJukebox and RealPlayer at RealNetworks. Elman holds a BS in symbolic systems with a focus on human computer interaction from Stanford University.

JOSH, TELL ME ABOUT YOURSELF. HOW DID YOU GET TO THE INFLUENTIAL POSITION YOU HAVE NOW?

When I was in college, I had on my résumé that my objective was to make great products that change people's lives. It's a weird statement for someone coming out of college, but I always knew I wanted to find companies and people doing things that could be a big part of the future, and help make them. I didn't ever aspire to start a company or be a founder; I really wanted to find things that could have a huge impact on the world and be a part of those things. So I've spent my entire career trying to do that. I started thinking that to really make an impact, you have to code and actually make stuff. I'd helped other people make stuff, but I had never made stuff. So I took my first job after college as an engineer at a company called RealNetworks, in Seattle. I worked on this thing called RealPlayer, which was the first way to view audio and video on the internet. In a couple of years, I was running a team of about fifteen engineers and product folks, shipping this RealPlayer client to hundreds of millions of people. It was pretty amazing.

Everything I've done now has been trying to chase my way back to my first job, shipping something that has an impact on hundreds of millions of people and changing the way they use technology. From Real, I went on to LinkedIn. We were fifteen people, and we were trying to figure out how to connect professionals so they would have more opportunity and more access to their jobs. We wanted to make it so opportunities would find them.

I got excited about a company called Zazzle, which was a marketplace that lets companies connect and build products on demand. If you had designs, you could upload them and have products shipped out the next day, without holding a bunch of inventory. I did that for a few years.

In 2008, I joined Facebook, because I really believed that, even in 2008, it was at such an early part of its journey on connecting all people in the world, and being the platform upon which all other services built in order to be social. I knew that the entire web and internet, applications and phone would all become more social. I worked on a platform there called Facebook Connect.

In fall of 2009, I joined Twitter. The company was just over eighty people, and Twitter in 2009 was known as this thing people used, but they weren't sure why. We figured out how to get the world on Twitter. I started a team there called Onboarding, which became User Growth. We figured out how to get our user base to a hundred million users and help people realize how Twitter could be more meaningful in their lives.

I left in 2011, because that work was in good shape. Rather than picking a company to join full-time, I tried to find a role where I could help more than one company at a time get to the same level. The idea of working with a venture firm seemed like a good job for me. I had worked with the guys at Greylock in the early days of LinkedIn, so I joined them. My full-time job now is as an investor, trying to find those companies that are at the early stages of forming really powerful networks and marketplaces. I consider investing in them as really trying to convince them to hire us. If they hire us, our job is to help them finish that journey to becoming a huge and successful company.

WHEN YOU THINK ABOUT WHAT YOU'VE DONE AT THOSE COMPANIES—HELPING EACH COMPANY BECOME SUCCESSFUL, MAKE GREAT PRODUCTS, AFFECT A LOT OF PEOPLE—HOW DO YOU DO THAT? WHAT'S THE STRATEGY FOR THAT?

There's no one-size-fits-all strategy. There are no shortcuts. You typically start with something that seems like it can make an impact. Someone has a great idea. The process of turning that idea into one of these companies is a process of finding out what that foundation is, what that really unique asset is, so, once you have it and build it, things cascade from there and you are really defensible and hard to displace. Often we call this the "network effect." Every new person who joins or starts using the service makes it much more valuable to everyone else on the service.

Not everything has a network effect that gets big. Some things get big as people store more data in them; this is called *progressive commitment*. You put more data in the system and you become more and more committed to the system over time. It gets harder and harder to leave that service. Evernote or Dropbox are great examples. Once you have a bunch of information on those services, it's much harder to leave. Google just gets better when more and more people use it, even though there isn't a discrete network effect. As you search more, Google's results get better, and as more people search and get better results, everyone wins.

The goal is identify the unique, foundational asset that you'll build around. Then you figure out how you can get as many people to pile on to that as quickly as possible, and to pile on in a meaningful way. If people really use the service in a meaningful way, through a network effect or progressive commitment, you end up with this potential for a really long-lasting system.

HOW DO YOU IDENTIFY THE DEFENDABLE ASSET?

For consumer companies, I look for one of two things. I look for attention, where you are aggregating people's energy. They are coming to you for information that they aren't getting elsewhere. Being that primary source of attention is critical. I also look for a foundational value. These are things like "safety and security of my things, whether it's my data or my ideas." Or "opportunities to find a new job, to make sure you can feed your family."

THOSE FOUNDATIONAL VALUES SEEM LIKE REALLY DEEP HUMAN QUALITIES, NOT LIKE THE TRIVIALITIES OF "MAKING A BETTER TO-DO LIST" OR "MAKING SEARCH EASIER TO USE." HOW HAVE YOU HONED YOUR ABILITY TO THINK ABOUT THOSE THINGS? IS THAT SOMETHING YOU CAN STUDY IN SCHOOL?

It is, kind of. You learn this type of thing in programs of psychology and sociology, not necessarily in computer science departments. I had this really lucky major at Stanford called symbolic systems, which also turned out people like Reid Hoffman of LinkedIn and Marissa Mayer of Google (and now Yahoo). They did the same major. The founder of Instagram, Mike Krieger, did it too. It's a combination of computer science, philosophy, linguistics, and psychology. It's a study of the layer, interface, or membrane of how people think of computers and how they interact.

But it also comes down to instinct. The hardest part of building something comes down to this: are you building it for yourself, or are you building it for how you believe most people will react and interact? It's important and really powerful to get out of your own head and think about how other people will engage with a system or a product, and make sure you are making choices that are meaningful to them, not to you. If you spend enough time asking the right questions, you have a pretty good chance of learning that instinct.

THAT'S A TACTICAL COMPETENCY IN BUILDING, BUT AN EMPATHETIC COMPETENCY IN PEOPLE.

That's exactly right. What's really changed, over the past five or ten years, is that computer systems have become much less about the *can you build it* and *how does it actually work*, and much more about *what should you build to change human behavior*. That means there's much more of an emphasis on *what is being built,* as compared to *how.* Google is the last company that got big in the computer technology industry simply because of what it could make computers do. Everything since then, Facebook, Twitter, Zynga, Groupon—all these companies are based on these much simpler principles of how people interact. Figure out the interface layer first. The technology comes later.

SO WHAT IS PRODUCT MANAGEMENT, IF IT'S NOT ANSWERING THE "CAN YOU BUILD IT" QUESTION?

The job is to help your team ship the right product to your users. A lot of people think product management is about being the CEO of the product, being the person who gets to make the decisions and drive the road map. I think that's patently wrong. I don't think the product manager is the CEO, or the decision maker, or the decider for a product. Great product managers help their team do those things. The product manager doesn't own the road map; the product manager *produces* the road map, based on the consensus conversations with design, engineering, and business. The product manager doesn't own the spec; he produces it based on conversations with everyone who is working on the product. They are responsible for capturing that in a document.

Your job is to help your team ship the right product to your users. Your job is to figure out who your users are, what they want to be able to do, and what the right products are to help them do that. Your job is to get the whole team to build those products. One way you can get them to do that is to set a crazy vision and have everyone rally around it and decide that it's awesome. You can do that by having your founder set the vision, and you just get the team to follow him. Draw something on a napkin and get everyone super-excited about it. But your job isn't to force them to do it. You need to sell, engage, learn, and listen, and get the whole team excited to go do it.

You also need to be a good storyteller. Great product managers can tell a story about a user, what he is doing in his life today, and what he would be able to do in the future if we just got him the right product. The story isn't necessarily about exactly what the product is—like, "it's a phone that's 4 inches by 3 inches." It's more like, "imagine if someone was walking down the street, got a buzz in his pocket, pulled out this device, and was able to see this information." You don't have to identify exactly what the features are to tell that story.

You need to be a great listener as well. You have to listen to everybody, absorb their wants and needs and ideas, and articulate a better story. You have to have humility. Because the entire process of building products is so full of trial and error and so full of mistakes that actually being humble is key to engaging a team. It's a confident humility, which I realize is an oxymoron. You have to be confident in what you believe in, but humble in what you are learning and listening to. It's really tricky. You can try to be Steve Jobs and be so sure you're right, but there's only one Steve Jobs. We all want to be Mark Zuckerberg, but there's only one Zuck. I get to work with people like Steve or Zuck and help them realize that new reality.

It's not just listening to people. It's also listening to data. You have to not just listen to what people say and their ideas, but also listen to data and queries, and try to figure out what people are doing by observing their behavior. It's not that you avoid making decisions, as if "the data says this, so we must do this." But you use it to inform yourself.

You also have to be creatively pragmatic. You have to be able to see what you want to get done and have creative ways to approach it with your team, but be pragmatic and understand how long things take, and what the actual dependencies are. You need to be creative around that reality in order to get something actually done and shipped.

WHERE DO PEOPLE ACQUIRE THOSE TRAITS?

The funny thing about product management is that there's no defined path. You have to sit at the nexus of all of those things I mentioned. I was recently speaking at a product conference where none of the other speakers had technical backgrounds. They came from drama, theater, and TV writing backgrounds. You can be a good storyteller, be creatively pragmatic, and have the right confident humility, no matter where you come from. The real question is, can you put these things together in a way to work with the hard nuts and bolts of engineering?

WHAT DOES A PRODUCT MANAGER DO?

It's less about what you do and more about what artifact you make. The engineer's artifact is code. The marketer's artifacts are ads, commercials, videos, and content. The product manager's artifact is the consensus road map and spec, and the position document that everyone uses to do those other two things well.

There are really four artifacts that a product manager makes. One is an overall road map that outlines the key initiatives that you want to take on to move the product forward. This is at a high level and describes your various goals. The spec is the second artifact, the detailed definition of the feature or change to the product that you'll make for any item in the road map. The third artifact is a positioning statement that you'll use to describe the thing to users. Amazon writes a press release before it builds the product. It can just be a few bullet points, but it explains why it is making this feature. It includes some metrics to measure the success of the feature. The last artifact is the detailed project plan, the steps the engineers say they need to go through to get the thing built.

HOW DO THOSE ARTIFACTS FIT IN WITH LEAN, AGILE, OR THE OTHER DEVELOPMENT MOVEMENTS THAT SEEM TO CATCH ON WITHIN PRODUCT CIRCLES?

Constantly refreshing your tactics and how you approach a solution to the problem is a good idea. But what those methodologies miss is that you have to set a vision, a North Star, or a key problem you are trying to solve. Then you use one of those methods to find the solution to the problem. Some preach that lean and agile are a way to go in search of a problem for customer development. I don't buy that as a way to get to innovation for consumer products. Maybe in a B2B context, because you do that back and forth to get to what the B2B customer needs in the market and is willing to pay for. But for consumers, you have to have more of a vision, something like, "Wouldn't it be great if this was how the world works?"

CAN YOU GIVE ME AN EXAMPLE OF HOW THE ARTIFACTS AND THE VISION ALL FIT TOGETHER?

When I was at Twitter, we identified a big problem. People would sign up for Twitter and never come back. They didn't quite get it. We had a secondary problem, too. We showed new users a suggested user list that had about a thousand people randomly presented for new users to follow. It was having a negative impact on the network, because those thousand people had a lot more followers than new people signing up. Everyone else in the network felt they were at a disadvantage, because they weren't part of that selected set.

So we had these two problems—the network wasn't happy, because people were getting favored, and new users were following random people who they didn't know. So the first project we did was to rebuild the whole flow in a way that was much more user-controlled, and it allowed us to train new users in how to use Twitter so that, over time, it became a more meaningful product for them to use.

We took the existing two-step process (find your friends, and then look at twenty random people that we suggest you follow), and we made it a three-step process. First, users browse categories across a bunch of topics and figure out who they want to follow within those categories. Then they find their friends—that was second because we thought the new categories were more important than finding friends. The third step was a catchall: "Did we miss anybody? You can search right here and find people you might have heard of on Twitter before you get started." That last search step was used by over 50 percent of the people signing up. When you're finished and you are back in Twitter, you've followed people along the way, so you are more likely to be set up better.

We were surprisingly successful. More people completed the flow, even though it was three steps instead of two. More people were engaged a month after going through that flow, and all that noise about advantaging people because they were included in the top one thousand went away.

IN THAT EXAMPLE, HOW DID YOU GET FROM NOTICING A PRODUCT PROBLEM TO COMING UP WITH THAT PARTICULAR SOLUTION?

I talked to people about what they thought Twitter was for and heard consistent things. Most people were saying, "I have a bunch of friends on it. It's for listening to your friends."

But my belief was that Twitter was about more than that. When we asked people what Twitter was for, I really wanted them to say that "it's about finding great content, or following your friends, or finding stuff around you." So we started building the flow, and we said, "That's how we'll organize the flow." We showed people mock-ups of it and said, "Now what do you think Twitter is for?" and they started telling us that it's for content, or friends, or finding new stuff.

We gave them a story to tell through the product itself, and then we got to a place where it felt right, so we shipped it. And it worked.

IT SEEMS AS IF, TO YOU, THE JOB IS ABOUT STORYTELLING MORE THAN ANYTHING ELSE.

I've always been a bit of a talker, and I was never as excited by how a computer works as I was by how it works *for people*. The engineering is necessary. But it's not sufficient. History is full of products that were possible to build, and were built, but were not the right products for users to use.

BECAUSE THE MARKET WASN'T READY?

No, it isn't that the market wasn't ready. It's that the product team wasn't reading the trends of the current time correctly. A part of product management is understanding how to take the right steps to build something forward. A lot of people don't always know how to break stuff down into discrete bits before moving on to the next thing. When I hear the timing was wrong or the market wasn't there, I think of it more like, "You didn't figure out how to ship to the *current* market and world."

Google Glass is a good example. My belief about Google Glass is that it feels right in the long run, but too early in the short run. If you are measured on making money on Google Glass in two years, you may not be successful. If this is a five-year play and they keep iterating, it's a smart play: "Let's charge a lot for the device, so only super 'fanbois' will buy it now."

My instinct is that something is there that is powerful and different, and feels like the future—like a way we would want to work, and that would natively feel pretty good and feel natural. Glass is impressive. But think about all the social norms, all the shifts, and all the other things that need to happen to make it feel like a normal behavior, and it doesn't feel like something that will be growing like wildfire a year from now. Google will sell a few, and a few more, and it will iterate, and the product will get better. Then by version three or four, people will be saying, "You don't have this yet? You are missing out."

THAT STORY YOU JUST TOLD ABOUT BEHAVIOR, THE FUTURE, AND ADOPTION—IS THAT HOW YOU GENERALLY THINK THROUGH PRODUCT DECISIONS?

Yes. You can see it for Facebook. All the college kids were on it, and you could say that someday most adults would be on it. A few got on, and a few more, and then suddenly people felt as if they were missing out if they weren't on it. Twitter was the same way. I got on Twitter in 2009, and some people are just starting to use it now.

WHAT ADVICE WOULD YOU GIVE TO SOMEONE WHO IS JUST STARTING OUT AND WANTS A CAREER IN PRODUCT MANAGEMENT?

My advice is to go work on something that is growing fast to scale, where it's still early enough that you can understand the decisions being made and how they are being made to scale, but not so early that you are trying to figure out on your own if it works. Examples of this today, in 2013, would be Pinterest, Dropbox, Airbnb, Square, or Uber. These companies don't have clearly defined successful business models, but they're not so new that they lack product-market fit.

In these companies, you would get the chance to learn what this type of scale is. You would be making decisions that touch a lot of people. If you go to companies that are too large, there is a small window for product development and you don't get to see how decisions affect the growth and trajectory of the product. But if you go too early, you are just trying to build the thing in the first place, and unless you are successful doing that, you haven't learned any lesson on building momentum.

So go find a hyper-growth company and learn. Then you'll spend your entire career chasing back to it. I got really lucky at RealNetworks, and I learned some great lessons. That helped me knock on LinkedIn's door. I wrote a letter, "Dear Reid and Eric—I did the same major as you at Stanford. I spent six years in Seattle, shipping RealPlayer to hundreds of millions of people. I love what you are doing. Is there any way I can help?" I learned how to scale, and that helped me get in the front door.

behavioral insights
identifying latent needs and desires

Joe is only half-listening to Mary, the chief marketing officer, as she verbally replays the last few hours. The two are walking back to the office after completing their first research session. They've spent two hours watching a yoga instructor prepare for her classes. This is part of the research program Joe outlined, because he wants to understand the ecosystem of health and wellness. Going into the research, his focus was on personal tracking and personal management, and he thought the yoga instructor would teach them about how to track the impacts of yoga on the body. Instead, they learned almost exclusively about mental health. They watched the instructor help a participant through a near-panic attack before the class started, and the entire thrust of the conversation among the class participants was on minimizing anxiety and fostering mental well-being. It didn't go at all as he expected. Joe is bemused.

In chapter 2, you learned that product-market fit is about broad community trends and market forces. In this chapter, we'll focus on behavioral insights, which are about individual behaviors. This means zooming in. Instead of analyzing how big companies are changing and why large market shifts are occurring, or thinking about whole communities of users, behavioral insights examine how one person interacts (or wants to interact) with your product to achieve his or her goals and aspirations.

Imagine this interaction as a dialogue, as if your product is literally having a conversation with a person. In a way, your product really *does* have this conversation, but it's abstract. When someone uses a product, she responds to the sum of interface design, aesthetics, and the product story. Her response is to further interact with the product, so a cyclical interaction occurs, back and forth. The space in which this abstract conversation occurs is human behavior.

Gaining behavioral insight is surprisingly simple. You'll need to spend time with the people who are going to use your product and watch them do whatever it is they do. Your goal is to both *understand them* and *empathize with them*. You can accomplish this by absorbing and interpreting signals, but unlike market signals that are broad and shared, these signals are local, discrete, and specific.

OBSERVING HUMAN BEHAVIOR

Often, the most difficult part of learning about people is determining which people to learn about. Our fictional character Joe is introducing a lifestyle product for tracking personal health information. He could quite literally hang around with anyone and learn something useful. But how can he optimize his rarest commodity, time, so he learns the most from the fewest?

The key is segmentation, but the segment that Joe is looking for is not based on demographics or those funky marketing psychographics. Instead, he's going to sort potential participants based on his ability to *watch real behavior*. In a way, he's less interested in the people themselves than in what they do, and that should be your lens, too. Observing human behavior in real time is the key to arriving at a product innovation that will drive engagement. This is different from observing or hearing about human behavior in retrospect, in general, or in hypothetical. You aren't conducting interviews or focus groups, which tend to discuss what people might do, ought to do, or typically do. Instead, you are watching what people *actually* do.

To determine which behavior to watch, build a profile that catalogs your *assumptions of existing behavior*. Describe these things within your product space:

- What do you think people currently do?
- Why do you think that?
- Where do you think people do it?
- How frequently do you think they do it?
- When do you think they do it?

Let's try it from Joe's perspective. (See table 3-1.)

Acknowledge, up front, that you are probably wrong about your answers to the profile questions. Being right or wrong is irrelevant because you now have a behavioral profile against which you can start to plan a research program, and you have a place to start. Rather than watching just anyone, you can go watch someone very specific: someone exercising at a yoga studio on her lunch break or after work. When you go to recruit this person, you may be surprised to find that there aren't any yoga classes at lunch, or, as Joe

Table 3-1

Joe's profile of people's existing behavior

What do you think people currently do?	I think people exercise a lot and track their progress in a methodical way, in a notebook or journal.
Why do you think that?	I saw someone write something in a notebook once, at my gym.
Where do you think people do it?	I think people do this tracking at the gym or at a structured class like yoga or Pilates.
How frequently do you think they do it?	I think people exercise two or three times a week and log their progress each time.
When do you think they do it?	I think they do the exercise on their lunch break or after work.

learned, people aren't tracking anything during their workouts. But that's OK. This is a starting point for you to start tracking signals of behavior.

SEEKING SIGNALS FROM PEOPLE

Behavioral research is aimed at identifying insight and occurs in a particular context. The context can be physical, geographic, or conceptual. For example, you may want to learn about how work is done in a particular business in order to optimize a process or work flow. Or, you might want to learn about the way a different culture engages with a particular technological advancement, such as mobile phone use in developing countries. Your research goal may be to understand or it may be to empathize, and the two aren't the same.

GAINING EMPATHY AND UNDERSTANDING

Understanding is about gaining knowledge. You may have no knowledge of a particular context—say, microfinance in South Africa—because you've never experienced it in your daily life. If you've never read about it, encountered it, or discussed it, there's no reason to think you can design to support it, so the role of behavioral research in this case is to learn. When the goal is to learn, the research output will typically be factual statements: *This is how the system works today. These are the people that make up the system. These are the tools and artifacts being used.* These factual statements can identify design opportunities—*these are the places where design can help*—and these opportunities are often called the "low-hanging fruit" of design.

Empathy is about acquiring feelings. The goal is to feel what it's like to be another person. That goal is kind of strange, because it's unachievable. To feel what someone else feels, you would need to actually become that person. You can approximate her feelings, so product research intended to build empathy is really about trying to feel what other people feel. Assuming you aren't actually an eighty-five-year-old woman, consider for a second what it *feels like* to be an eighty-five-year-old woman. This *consideration* is still analytical: it's about understanding. You need to get closer to experiencing the same emotions that an eighty-five-year-old woman experiences, so you need to put yourself into the types of situations she encounters.

What does it feel like to drive, given the various physical changes that the human body encounters when it gets old? You could role-play, like an actor, and that would get you closer to feeling what an older driver might experience. You could actually go driving with an eighty-five-year-old, and this would get you closer to feeling what she feels. You could go so far as to impair your vision (say, wear glasses rubbed with Vaseline) and augment your body (by taping your fingers at the knuckles to simulate arthritis) to be more like that of an eighty-five-year-old, and that would get you still closer to building empathy. The more of these exercises you do, the closer you can approximate her feelings, leaving your own perspective in order to temporarily take on hers.

When you're old, what does it feel like to read the paper? What does it feel like to use e-mail? What does it feel like to go to the doctor? You can answer these questions by getting closer to the actual behavior of the elderly reading the paper or using e-mail or going to the doctor. The output will be hard to explain to someone else, because feelings are personal and complicated. While you can write detailed requirements and use cases about things you understand, it's particularly difficult to tell someone else about things you feel.

The split here between understanding and empathy is overly reductive, made only to illustrate the distinctions. In reality, most product research is about both understanding and empathizing at once, and in the context of learning, experience contributes to both. When you look to gain signals from behavior, you are looking for both what people do and how they feel.

GATHERING BEHAVIORAL SIGNALS

The process for gathering these types of behavioral signals is surprisingly simple. You need to be in the place where the behavior actually happens. You need to watch the behavior happen. And you need to talk to the people who are doing it. *That's all there is to it.* There's no survey or prepared focus group. You simply have a conversation with someone, while he performs some sort of activity or takes some action.

A conversation with a stranger can be a little, well, strange. There are ways to minimize the social awkwardness, which I describe later, and you'll find that most people are delighted to talk about what they do and feel all day because typically no one ever asks them. Your interest in observing the minutia of their behavior shines a spotlight on their life and makes them feel special.

The following steps explain how to gather behavioral signals by watching people do something and talking to them while they do it.

Establish and articulate a focus.

Before you go into the behavioral context, establish a focus. A focus is a succinct description of the scope of your behavioral research. Your focus might be to learn about the way people use and think about banking services, to watch the way orders are placed at a given business, or to see what it's like for families to go to the movies. Your focus will help you identify the appropriate context for your research. It will help you build the behavioral profile described earlier so you can select people to visit. And it will help you steer your conversation during the actual research session.

Prepare a series of set questions, but try not to use them.

Develop a set of ten open-ended, broad questions that clarify your focus. These should be questions about actions, work flow, and processes, not about statistics or opinions. If possible, these questions should actually provoke behavior. See tables 3-2 and 3-3 for some good and bad questions.

Developing this list of questions serves several purposes. First, it forces you to mentally role-play how the actual research will go, and it gives you a chance to form a mental representation of the behavior you will observe. Next, it primes you to ask these types of questions naturally as you see opportunities during your research session. Finally, it gives you a backup plan if the participant just isn't forthcoming with action. You can always turn your research into an interview, simply asking questions and hearing responses. This isn't ideal, but it's better than wasting time and resources.

Table 3-2

Good questions for clarifying focus

GOOD QUESTIONS TO ASK:	THIS IS A GOOD QUESTION BECAUSE:
Can you show me how you use the software to process that order?	The question provokes action and directs the conversation toward reality rather than hypothetical situations.
What's your least favorite part of shopping at this store? Can you show me why you don't like it?	People are typically able to describe negative feelings, and the participant can recreate the problem.
Can you remember a time when your vehicle broke? Can you show me what part broke?	People can often remember specific, bad situations. The participant can use the physical vehicle as a prop to recreate a story with action.

Table 3-3

Bad questions for clarifying focus

BAD QUESTIONS TO ASK:	THIS IS A BAD QUESTION BECAUSE:
Do you like this product?	It's not relevant to a particular quest for behavioral signals, and it's a nonstarter: it's easy to answer yes or no, and offer no additional details.
Which three features do you use the most? How much time do you spend using them?	People have a hard time monitoring their own usage patterns and have difficulty estimating frequency of events. Additionally, this question makes it easy to avoid actually *doing* anything: this doesn't transition the user to action.
If we designed something to fix this problem, would you buy it?	Hypothetical purchasing behavior is simply not believable, as actual purchasing behavior depends on so many interconnected issues (price, aesthetics, timing, etc.). This type of conjecture doesn't get any closer to observing behavior.

Get in context, and record everything.

Doing your behavioral research in the actual environment in which the behavior typically occurs is critical. You might be tempted to bring participants into a neutral place, like an office or a coffee shop, and have them offer a retrospective summary of a given activity. But you don't want a retrospective, and you really don't want a summary. You want a rich, cohesive, detailed, and real view into the person's personal life or job. This means that you'll need to find your way into that special context, which can be challenging. You can't just show up at an air traffic control tower and expect to hang out for the day. Instead, contextual research requires scheduling and networking prior to your visit. It also demands a level of respect, particularly when you enter someone's home or business, and a particular reverence for personal space.

When you are in context, capture the experience. Get permission from your participant to record and then use an audio recorder to capture what is said. Take pictures. Shoot video. Try to capture as many artifacts as possible, so you can synthesize the data later.

Ask to see examples.

When the participant mentions a product, process, work flow, piece of software, or any other noun or verb, ask to see an example. This grounds the conversation in action. Instead of talking about the software, ask to see your participant use it. Instead of hearing about some process she has to go through every day, ask her to show it to you. Simply asking, "Can I see an example?" can help you gain a great deal of insight and clarity.

Ask to try it.

When you find yourself observing a novel situation, ask to try it yourself. For example, if you are watching a butcher prepare meat, ask if you can make a few cuts. If you are observing a college teacher grade papers, ask if you can grade some. You haven't lost anything if the person says no.

But if he says yes, you'll be pushing closer to empathy by gaining valuable experience, and you'll have converted your participant into a teacher. A good teacher will help you learn.

Watch at the extremities.

Try to watch behavior that's at the extremities or that's highly unique. This might mean watching six or seven different people, and trying to recruit extremely different types of participants in different contexts. Look for failures or events that don't work. Try to find anomalies or outliers, people who have extraordinary views or attitudes. These anomalies present new, provocative frames, and they can be useful in helping you see the world in a new way.

LEARNING FROM SIGNALS OF PRODUCT USAGE

If you have an existing product, you can gather signals from how people are using it. You can do this specifically—watching a single person use your product—or in aggregate, to learn how the entire population of users is interacting with it.

You can learn about broad product usage patterns by examining analytics data. This data is generated through various discrete events (people click there or push that button when they encounter that screen) or by a flow of events in a sequence (after encountering this, people typically go over there). This type of data is interesting because it highlights opportunities for change. It might, for example, call attention to a part of a sequence where many people change their minds. Or, it might tell you that a certain button is much more likely to be clicked than another button.

What this type of aggregate data *doesn't* tell you, however, is *why*. You'll know something is performing well or isn't performing at all, but it will be up to you to infer causality between the behavior patterns you observe and specific product decisions.

You can complement this broad view of product usage with very specific one-on-one evaluation data in order to identify the *why*. One of the simplest ways to understand this is to conduct a formal think-aloud usability test, with a task structured around the broad pattern you've observed. In this style of usability test, a user is asked to work to achieve a goal while *thinking out loud*. This means that he verbalizes what he is doing as he does it; the facilitator doesn't interrupt him or, as is the case in other evaluation techniques, ask him about his feelings. Instead, the facilitator is there only to prompt the user to keep talking.

This helps the facilitator understand why the user is doing what he is doing as he makes decisions. If you observe a strange usage pattern in product data and then formalize a usability test around that usage pattern, you'll be able to understand why a person is making various decisions. Your small-sample usability test won't be statistically significant, but it will help you better interpret the large-scale pattern you are observing. It will provide you with a robust set of product-usage signals.

The methods I've discussed for discovering signals into behavior share something in common. They require you to interact with the people who will be using your product in an intimate fashion. You can't hide behind an online survey and expect to gain empathy with people. You need to spend time with them, laugh with them, experience their highs and lows, and get to know them. These methods can be intimidating, but shouldn't be. I find that intimidation comes from how unfamiliar these methods feel. Our jobs typically keep us in front of computer screens, abstracting the rest of the world to a set of faceless data. This process forces you out of your office and into real life, which is chaotic, textured, and exciting. Hopefully, as the intimidation of contextual research wears off, you can find pleasure in the act of learning how other people live their lives.

FRAMEWORKS TO SYNTHESIZE BEHAVIORAL INSIGHTS

Joe has run out of wall space. He laughs to himself. Based on his experience, it's a good problem to have.

Every surface is covered with quotes. The team has transcribed the research, verbatim, and Joe showed them how to explode the research into individual utterance cards. Now, the twelve research participants are no longer individually recognizable because they are blended into a sea of research data. There are large categories of comments on the wall, and each category is labeled. A giant printout in all block letters reads, "PEOPLE NEED TO UNDERSTAND THEIR EMOTIONS OVER TIME; GIVE THEM A WAY TO VISUALIZE THE EMOTIONAL." Another reads, "HEALTH IS A STORY THAT UNFOLDS OVER TIME. HELP PEOPLE TELL THEIR STORY."

The team members are all here, looking around. Joe gets the sense that they are literally marinating in the work they've produced. There's silence. He doesn't disturb it.

Previously, you read about observing the world around you, at a communal level of the market and at a local level of the individual. Observing the world around you is the fastest way to gather signals about people's behavior. But observation gives you only a part of the story: it shows you what people did, but not why they did it. These observations give you lots of data, but the data is lacking contextual depth, so it stops short of providing you information or knowledge. It still doesn't answer the hardest question: what should I build? You can gain the contextual depth necessary to answer this question through rigorous interpretation.

INTERPRETING TO IDENTIFY NEEDS

Interpretation will help you identify needs or areas where people are underserved by current products or service. This identifies very clearly what should be created in order to satisfy the need. For example, if you observe people using the subway, you'll see a number of flaws in the ticket-purchasing process that could be improved by design. Tourists may not understand the process, so they may spend a disproportionate amount of time at the ticket kiosk. This tells you that the process is too difficult for first-time users. People may juggle their coffee, mobile phone, and wallet. This tells you that the kiosk needs a surface for people to put things on. There is little inference between your observations and your interpretations, so you can think of these as safe interpretations. Put another way, the observation identifies both the problem and the solution. Since the gap between problem and solution is small, innovation risk is small, too.

INTERPRETING TO IDENTIFY INSIGHTS

Interpretation will also identify insights, which are provocative statements of truth about people that speak to their lifestyle choices, their aspirations, and their desires. For example, if you observe people using the subway, you'll see some people working on their laptops and other people reading books or newspapers. You can interpret this behavior in a number of ways. You might guess that people want to be left alone. The boundaries of public and private space are confused in such tight confines, so artificial items like books or headphones create artificial walls to delineate space. Or, you might guess that people are celebrating the focus they've achieved. The confines of the space force them to be more productive. Both interpretations make sense, and both will lead you in different directions, but there is a large amount of inference between your observations and these interpretations. Your observation identifies neither a problem nor a solution, so innovations that are based on these interpretations will carry risk.

Transcribe, externalize, and build the product synthesis wall.

A product synthesis wall is an invaluable tool to help you "get the research out"—out of your head and also out of your laptop. Your goal is to produce an external, tactile, collaborative, and highly visual representation of all of the research. There's a simple reason why externalization of the data is important. When you store things in your computer, you'll find yourself organizing data in a way that makes sense to those who designed the software you are using. You'll put things in files and folders, and as a result, you'll produce a highly hierarchical and analytical organization of the data. You'll also lose the ability to understand the research in its breadth, and you will find yourself limited in your ability to form connections across data.

That's the preliminary goal of the synthesis wall: to discover hidden connections between individual utterances or actions, and to see anomalies or outliers in a large bulk of data. The wall forces you to see the data in a new way and to question your preconceived understanding of hierarchy, relationships, and causality.

Jon Freach, director of design research at frog design, gave me three reasons why the externalization of data is critical for successful innovations: "First, the physicality of a dedicated room gives the project team a common space to work together in. Second, the room says to the organization, 'this is important work' and through its structure conveys an evolving narrative about what the team is learning and making. At any point in time, stakeholders can 'read the room' and walk away informed or inspired. The third, and possibly most useful function of a room filled with externalized data, is that it enables forced comparison of information and team dialogue to occur—two critical and often overlooked tools in a designer's toolbox, both of which are essential to the act of sensemaking."

The primary input for your synthesis wall will be behavioral research— the research where you watched people do things, like work or play. Start by transcribing each of those research sessions in its entirety. This is extremely tedious. You'll be tempted to make your intern do it. Resist the temptation. Buck up and do it yourself, because transcription is an *extraordinarily important part of this process of learning.* As you type, word for word, what you heard and saw, you'll find yourself reliving the experience and achieving a sort of meta-analysis of what each person said. You'll find yourself constantly asking *why*. Why did they say that, and what did they really mean? It will probably take you about four times longer to transcribe a session than it took you to actually do the research, as you'll constantly rewind and pause the recording. But, slowly, you'll have a verbatim transcript of the research, capturing the signals you learned from the various people you talked to. You'll also quite literally hear the participants' voices in your head, and you'll be better able to respond to design ideas from their perspective, as if you were channeling their opinions. Most importantly, you'll have integrated the interview contents into your worldview, and you'll think about the problem space differently. The transcription process, and the subsequent synthesis process, is how you will make sense of data.

The transcription is a linear representation of one research participant. But in order to intermingle the results of *all* participants, you'll need to explode the research into a nonlinear, modular form. This way, you can move each quote or utterance around independently and start to find patterns and anomalies.

EXPLODING RESEARCH INTO A NONLINEAR FORM

Here's a very effective, geeky way to move from a standard written transcript to individual 2.75" x 4.25" notes that can be moved around, where each note is a quote from one of your research participants:

1. Copy the entire transcript from a participant and paste it into a spreadsheet. Each paragraph will become its own cell in the spreadsheet. Each cell is called an *utterance*.

2. Add a column in the spreadsheet with the initials of the participant (like JK), and another column with a unique identifier (1, 2, 3 . . .). This will help you backtrack to the exact moment in the research, once the research is no longer in a linear form.

3. Open a tool like Microsoft Word and find the mail merge or mailing label functionality—the ability to merge your spreadsheet into a series of labels. Add the various content blocks to the label: the utterance itself, the initials of the participant, and the unique identifier. Complete the merge, and you'll end up with a printable format of the transcript, with eight utterances per page.

4. Print the merged notes and cut the pages so you have individual notes for every utterance.

5. Place each note on the wall using pushpins or tape. You've effectively made the research nonlinear, because you can now move the notes around freely. Repeat this activity with all of the research participants, and you'll have several thousand unique notes on the wall. That's a good day's work, and at this point, you should take a break.

Identify patterns and anomalies.

Now you can begin to find patterns across the data. Read each note and, using a highlighter, indicate those things you find interesting. There's no need to rationalize what's interesting or try to place criteria around it, and it's perfectly acceptable that "interesting" is both subjective and inconsistent. You might highlight things that you find surprising or things with a particular emotional, financial, or logistical impact. Your frame of reference has been honed by the market signals you've been observing, so your brain already has a filter for picking out interesting things to highlight. Put another way, there's no wrong answer and lots of right ones.

As you move through the notes and highlight things that catch your attention, physically move the notes around to place similar ones next to each other. This similarity will span *across* interview participants, so over time you'll lose an understanding of any one research participant. As the notes start to mingle and merge, you'll find patterns that cut across research participants. As these patterns emerge, name them. Write a name on a colorful Post-it note that represents the *behavioral intent* of the grouping. Avoid names that are functional or overly abstract, like "Work flow" or "Governance." Instead, the names should be rich guesses about the culture, behavior, and norms like, "There seem to be extraordinarily ineffective processes used by all stakeholders" or "There are ways that the participants are emotionally hurting themselves."

Joe has returned from his research at the yoga studio and has grouped these quotes together:

> *"I'm just so tense all of the time. Yoga really helps me unwind . . . it's not just the yoga, actually, it's my friends here."*

"I don't normally eat like this, but you happened to catch me on a night with nothing in the fridge to cook and I had such a shitty day at work. Don't judge me, OK? [laughs]"

"When I get home, there's nothing left. This is me, sitting on the porch, drinking whiskey. That's all I got."

"I tried going to the gym in the afternoon [drops weights, takes a drink from drink bottle]. But I never had enough energy left, and I was always so pissed off from work that I would just skip it. And then I felt bad that I skipped it, and so I felt worse . . . it was a terrible cycle. The morning is better."

Joe grouped these together because each seemed negative—each described a bad feeling. It seemed to him that, at the end of the day, the participants had arrived in a poor mental space. They didn't say anything about their jobs, but all of them worked, so he labeled the group:

"People seem concerned by their stressful jobs, but they don't seem to do anything to fix their situations."

As you immerse yourself in the data, you'll naturally start to have product ideas. Write them down (use a single-color Post-it note to record ideas like this) but try not to spend too much time focusing on idea generation. Ideas are interesting, but at this stage, your goal is to both develop and extract insights about behavior. Fundamentally, you are trying to hone in on *why people do the things they do.*

This process typically takes one or more weeks. For eight to ten research participants, plan to spend twenty or thirty hours with the data. The process doesn't need to happen all at once, so you'll need a quiet place with a lot of wall space to conduct this activity.

Visualize behavior across time.

As you spend time with the data, you'll start to see details emerge that describe the experiences and activities you saw, as well as broader experiences that people described. These structures typically relate to work flow or lifestyle choices, and the time frame of these activities may span seconds (as a person tries to achieve a goal), or it may reference phases of someone's life or career.

As you become aware of the events that occur over time, draw them. Create a simple diagram on a whiteboard or a large sheet of butcher paper that shows the flow of data, emotions, and decisions across time. Use circles to indicate stages and lines with arrowheads to show the connection between stages. These diagrams aren't comprehensive, and there's no formal syntax to use when you make them. Your goal is to simply represent time-based behavior that you see in the data you've collected.

Make succinct observational statements.

Armed with your utterance groupings and your time-based visualizations, you can start the process of insight extraction by making succinct statements about the things you've observed. Recall Joe's observational statement from his research:

> *"People seem concerned by their stressful jobs, but they don't seem to do anything to fix their situations."*

First, note that the statement makes a sweeping generalization about the people he spoke with, but doesn't make any attempts to qualify the statement as biased. At this point, it's perfectly fine to be biased; in fact, bias is desired, because it implies a thoughtful depth of interpretation. When you interpret, you assign meaning to data. That assignment is a subjective process. At the same time, don't lose sight of your objective. You are trying to provoke something new, not predict how a small data set maps to a larger population. This is not a statistics exercise.

Next, note that the statement is an observation, not a solution. Joe doesn't offer a way to help these people yet, nor does he judge the contents. He simply makes a statement.

Finally, notice how the statement is subtly concerned with both behavior and time. It points out a state of mind (*being concerned*), as well as a causal chain that stretches over time (*being concerned might lead to fixing the concern*).

This observational statement is a bridge statement on the way to an insight. Create an observational statement about each group of utterances you've identified. You should end up with between eight and ten observational statements.

Extract insights.

Now, you can use the observational statements to extract insights. In the context of design and innovation, an insight is a provocative statement of truth about human behavior. Each statement is *presented* as a fact, but each is *actually* an inference. Each statement may be factually wrong, so using insights will introduce risk into your process, but this risk has its reward. Insights are the source of innovation: insights are gold. When you get a "hit" with an insight, you'll tap into some pretty powerful human motivators to help people change their behavior, and you'll be able to build these motivators into your products.

It's easy to move from a series of signals to an insight. Start with your observational statements. These statements are true, at least for the people you watched and the data you gathered, but are stated as true for a larger population. These statements become the foundation upon which insights are formed.

Now, ask and answer the question, "Why?" When you answer the question, you are making an inference. You've assigned meaning to the data that you gathered. Your inference may be wrong, because it's a guess.

Joe made this observational statement:

"People seem concerned by their stressful jobs, but they don't seem to do anything to fix their situations."

When Joe asks and answers the question, "Why?" he might arrive at any of the following inferences:

- People are trapped in a lifestyle that places high stress demands on their daily lives. They have financial obligations that make it impossible to quit their jobs.
- People are not actually burdened by the stress. Even though they are concerned about it, it's not actually affecting their lives in a meaningful way.
- People are generally aware of the stress in their jobs, but aren't specifically aware of the stress at any given moment or day. They feel the cumulative emotional burden of stress only after it's too late to do anything about it.

Each of these inferences is believable, yet each one could also be completely wrong. But each is stated as if it's a universal truth. A few data points have been generalized in order to make a broad statement about why people do the things they do. Joe—and you—will move forward *as if you've identified a causal relationship, even though you obviously haven't.*

Each statement takes an authoritative tone, even though each statement is not a valid inductive argument. These are insight statements. This authoritative tone makes it possible to use the insight as a point of departure to identify product constraints. Insights are about human behavior, as they describe intent, actions, emotions, and other aspects of motivation. Insights are provocative because they act as a logical gatekeeper: based on an insight statement, other things have to logically follow.

Joe selected the last statement:

- People are generally aware of the stress in their jobs, but aren't specifically aware of the stress at any given moment or day. They feel the cumulative emotional burden of stress only after it's too late to do anything about it.

Now, he can use the declarative statement to identify a product constraint. A product constraint defines the boundaries that dictate what the product or service should do, how it should act, and how it should feel.

- People are generally aware of the stress in their jobs, but aren't specifically aware of the stress at any given moment or day. They feel the cumulative emotional burden of stress only after it's too late to do anything about it. **There should be a way for people to see day-to-day changes in their stress, so they can constantly adjust their behavior in an ongoing fashion.**

This is a product constraint, and at a very high level, it tells Joe what to build. Insights do the work for you. Designing a desirable product isn't about having a good idea. It's about making insightful observations about existing behavior and transforming that behavior into a more desirable one.

Take a second to reflect on this process. It starts with local facts, observations that are individually true based on a tiny set of data. Next, it groups these observations and simultaneously makes assumptive and inferential leaps on top of the facts in order to make more global behavioral statements. Each leap is a step away from something we are sure about, so each leap is risky. This is the risk of innovation: it demands that someone make guesses about human behavior and not only make these guesses but build upon them. The larger the leap, the more likely it is to be wrong, but with a larger leap comes a more unexpected innovation, a more jarring, differentiated, and unique idea.

You'll also note that when moving from initial interpretation to insight, Joe introduced new knowledge and assumptions. These additions came from within Joe, and will come from within you. This acknowledges the role of experience. The more things you have experienced, the broader your palette of extra knowledge, the more you can build upon and refine interpretations in order to arrive at unique and useful insights.

An insight statement should feel simple, because it *is* simple. If you read an insight statement without having gone along for the ride that got there, you'll scratch your head and say, "That's it?" But you can't get to an insight without working your way through the complexity of behavior, connections, patterns, and people. The synthesis wall is complexity. It's hard. And it will feel hard, tedious, and time consuming. But the results that pop out the other side of synthesis are the elegant truths of innovation, grounded in their humanity and beautiful in their simplicity.

Communicate your results.

For a few reasons, you might want to communicate your understanding and empathizing to someone else. You might be on a team, and your goal is to create alignment on the findings. You might be a consultant, and your goal is to create a sea change for your client. Or you might be hunting for a job and you want to show that you are, in fact, qualified to drive new product vision. You might want to communicate *things that actually happened or that you actually saw*.

Typically, this is done in a spreadsheet or with bullet points on a slide, but a better way is through pictures, with quotes from real people. This provides both the context of an action or activity as well as a view of intent. What people say and what people do provide clues for *what people want to do* and *how people want to be*. Because it's not practical to communicate everything you saw—it would take too long—you must choose "this" over "that" and explain your choices. If you spent two hours in the field, you saw two hours of data. Why did you select five pictures to display? Was there something particularly interesting about them? Do they provide evidence of inefficiency? Evidence of a cultural norm that you want to highlight?

You also might want to communicate *things you actually felt*. These emotions are hard, but not impossible, to describe. Description alone is not going to be enough to really get other team members to feel what you felt. *I felt sad* doesn't capture the type of sadness and isn't rich enough for your team to share your feelings. Typically, emotions are best conveyed in some sort of time-based medium, because this provides the audience with a baseline and a point of comparison. The medium might be a video clip, a comic strip, a timeline, a series of photos, or some other way of showing a time-based narrative.

You might want to communicate *your interpretations of what happened and your interpretations of how you felt*. This is the assignment of meaning to the data. It's your introspection on *why things happened*. When you interpret, you'll begin to combine data in new ways; bring in external sources of data; and compare, contrast, and judge the data you gathered. Typically, this interpretation requires some form of visual diagramming—a map or a chart—to illustrate these forced and provocative connections.

Or, you might want to communicate *the implications of your interpretations of what happened and how you felt*. The implications act as design constraints and point toward new design ideas. I've found it most useful to illustrate these implications through sketches, as if to say, "This is the translation of data, gathered in the field, to *actionable design stuff*." Even if you are a product researcher and not an actual designer, this is still in your realm of job responsibility. People typically ignore a deck of slides with bullet points. A sketch will much more likely be used because it offers an incomplete vision of the future. The viewer can participate by completing the story in his or her mind.

In this chapter, you learned how to build empathy with an audience and how to extract meaningful insights from a sea of behavioral data. This step in the process is one way in which a design-led approach to product management is differentiated from an engineering or marketing approach; these insights are the big rocks upon which your product vision will be built. The process feels natural, because it *is* natural. People, not technology, are at the root of emotionally engaging products. This process is for talking to people and getting to know them; and it combines psychology and anthropology to uncover latent wants, needs, and desires. After completing this step, you'll be ready to build your product strategy. I'll show you how to do that in the next chapter.

- -

AN INTERVIEW WITH GARY CHOU,
ON THE SPIRIT AND SOUL OF PRODUCT DEVELOPMENT

- -

Gary Chou is a fun guy based in Brooklyn, New York. Most recently, Chou worked at Union Square Ventures, a New York City–based venture capital firm, where he created and managed the Union

Square Ventures Network of portfolio companies. Prior to joining Union Square Ventures in 2010, he held product roles at tech companies and start-ups.

He currently teaches entrepreneurial design at the School of Visual Arts, MFA in Interaction Design Program, and advises the Austin Center for Design, which exists to transform society through design and design education; and Venture for America, which seeks to revitalize American cities and communities through entrepreneurship.

In his work with independent creators, Chou produced *Surrogate Valentine* (SXSW 2011) and *Daylight Savings* (SXSW 2012), two films by Dave Boyle. He frequently collaborates with musician Goh Nakamura on web-related projects.

Chou has backed more than Kickstarter projects; he is an ordained minister of the Universal Life Church. He's currently working on what's next.

GARY, TELL ME ABOUT YOUR EXPERIENCES IN PRODUCT MANAGEMENT.

I got into product management around the early days of the internet and the first dot-com boom. That was a time when there wasn't a clear understanding of how you make web-based software, how you produce things, how you take advantage of the web. Most of the ways you produced stuff followed a shrink-wrapped software model, because that was all we knew. But I started working at an enterprise software company called Trilogy; it was launching a bunch of dot-com subsidiaries, one of which was to sell major appliances over the web. My function was trying to define what it was we did, trying to help make decisions based on constraints; it was, in effective, product management, even though I didn't know what to call it at that point. It was like herding cats. That was a small team, four or five people, and the company failed after two years.

I went back to Trilogy, where I worked on a product that didn't actually ship. Then I moved to California, where I spent a couple of years working on my own ideas. These ideas were about how you leverage the web to foster community. During that time, I didn't know that what I was doing was product management as well: I was going out, trying to understand a community of people, and trying to see how technology could be used to serve them. I was focused on the arts community in the Bay Area. This was before the web was social, before Friendster and MySpace existed. I was always interested in understanding people and how technology could be applied there; that's at the heart of what a product manager does.

Not until I joined a start-up called Tribe.net as a product manager did all of these things start to come together. I had the good fortune of working with Chris Law, who I met at Trilogy, who managed the group. I also worked with another guy from Trilogy named Elliot Loh, who was a product manager and designer at Tribe. That's when things started to formalize for me. Chris had a great background in product, having worked at Microsoft before, and had a way of managing process and managing us through releases; he had a certain discipline. Elliot brought a fantastic design sense, how to develop a language for the types of things we wanted to make. This was much more sophisticated schooling on how to make stuff. I was at Tribe for about two and a half years. The one thread I seem to have in my career, to some degree, is that I tend to work at companies that fail. When you are failing, that's when the processes matter, your assumptions are being challenged, you have to create better solutions, and you have to figure out what does or doesn't work.

That's beneficial. When you step into a position, and everything's going up and to the right and everything's working, you never really know *why* everything's working. I learned a lot about why things don't work when I was at Tribe. That was a great time to learn the ropes of product management. Ultimately, Cisco purchased the assets to Tribe and acquired the team, too. I joined Cisco around 2006.

At Cisco, I got a glimpse of what it was like to work at a big company. When you work at such a big company, you have access to the e-mail lists, to all the news, and the things that are going on in the larger entity. When I think about the product work I've done in a wide variety of circumstances, this was a very frustrating point in my life. Because, as a maker, you want things to work. When things don't work and you don't understand why, it can be paralyzing and frustrating. I was fortunate that at the peak of my frustration, I made contact with a venture capital firm in New York called Union Square Ventures. It was a small firm and had a growing portfolio, and recognized that the partners themselves—there were three at the time—couldn't scale up to handle the demands of their portfolio by themselves.

They recognized that they needed someone who had lived in that world, who had dealt with a fair share of pain, to try to help them. They hired me, so I moved from San Francisco to New York. The best part of that gig was that it gave me the space to reflect on all of those years of frustration in working on product. I was surrounded by great people. The partners at the firm are some of the best thinkers about the internet and networks, which has been my area of focus.

At a venture capital firm, you don't do quality assurance, support, or engineer anything; you put money in stuff. Simply being out of the role of having to make something freed up my brain to process all of the things I had done before. I was in a portfolio of fantastic companies that were successful, far more successful than anything I had worked on. It put me in a perfect place to observe what was working and to see why it was working. Until that point, I had taken a very unsophisticated approach to product management. When we made a lot of our design decisions at Tribe, it was through a functional lens. But when you are building social networks, you are primarily trying to design for people who are fundamentally irrational and who have feelings.

That's been my arc, from a product perspective. I've worked in the trenches in a lot of unsuccessful places and then moved to a very different field—venture—where I could reflect on it all.

GIVEN THAT REFLECTION, WHAT IS YOUR DEFINITION OF PRODUCT MANAGEMENT NOW?

I wonder if product management is just a label we've come up with because we don't have a better way of describing it. It means different things at different places. In some cases, people expect the head of product to drive the ship and to own the vision or the road map. Then you have lots of other cases where that vision is owned by the founders. There are other situations where everyone wants to drive the vision, and if they aren't on the same page, there's a lot of conflict.

Product management is the art of keeping everything moving together. It's a practice that ensures that a company or an organization or a group of people is making forward progress. If they aren't, there's something broken in how they approach features, or the prioritization, or their working processes. It usually falls on product management to figure out why it is broken and to make sure it doesn't happen. So I like to think about product management as a force within an organization that makes sure people are taking good swings at the plate. Where the vision comes from is highly variable.

It's an execution-oriented role. But I don't know if it's tactics and skills; I think it's etiquette and culture. We all have examples in our social circles of people who are just great with the group. They are comfortable managing the relationships of a complex group of people, and they have the respect of a disparate group of people. They can get people to work together. I can't think of an example of a great product manager who is a polarizing figure or is egocentric. As product manager, you are in charge of something, but you have no control. No one reports to you. So you can react to that in a few ways. You can pound your fists and say, "I need more control," but that's not really how you lead. There's a lot that has to happen, especially in a complex organization, so it feels like it's constantly moving forward. The person who steers the ship is not necessarily making it go forward. That's how I see the role. It's hard for me to think of a handbook with the list of tactics that are effective, because so much of it is personality driven.

IT'S INTERESTING TO THINK OF A ROLE THAT'S PRIMARILY DEFINED BY PERSONALITY TYPE. DOES IT BEG THE QUESTION: WHAT DOES A PRODUCT MANAGER ACTUALLY *DO*?

I would have answered the question very differently two years ago. When I first got to Union Square Ventures, I looked around at the portfolio companies and started to dig into how they made product decisions, what their processes were, and generally how they made product. All of the companies did it differently. In the back of my mind, I had a very naive reaction: I thought, "Well, you're doing it wrong, and you're doing it wrong, and you're doing it wrong . . ." I was very judgmental because of my experiences; I thought, "My ten years of experience had to count for something, right?" The truth is, none of it really mattered.

What mattered for these companies is not that they do things the way I like to do things, but that they each found a way to be effective, a process that adhered to the personality of the founders and the culture of the company, and they were able to make forward progress. So I would judge a process based on whether they were making progress or not. The process that works for one company may be completely unproductive in another company.

There are common traits shared by product managers. The idea of control goes out the window. The more tightly a product manager tries to control the situation, the less successful they will be. Another trait is the ability to ask good questions. If you can ask good questions, you can challenge things, because you are thinking deeply about the problem you are trying to solve, not because you are charismatically trying to assert your point of view on the team and on the world.

These types of things allow someone to be effective.

YOU MENTIONED TRAITS, AND IT SOUNDS AS IF CHARACTER OR PERSONALITY TRAITS ARE CONSISTENT ACROSS PRODUCT MANAGERS. CAN YOU LIST OR DESCRIBE WHAT THOSE ARE?

It's more complex than that. Many early-stage companies don't have a strong product lead, because sometimes those functions are subsumed in what the founders are doing. You could have highly product-oriented founders who would manage the process. You might have a head of engineering fluent in the whole process of managing a product release himself, so he may take on those roles, too. That's part of why I've retreated to this idea of trying to understand traits rather than functions, because the structure of these organizations doesn't look the same at all.

The people who end up playing the product role are closest to the problem they are trying to solve. For a lot of Union Square Venture's companies, the things they've invented aren't utilities. They can't write a product requirements document of "this is the product we are going after, here's the market, here's our rollout strategy." These founders have intuited a lot, which then led to this amazing thing. It's kind of like being a scientist and playing with a couple of free agents. Then it's like, "Whoa, I have a reaction now—this seems like a thing. And oh, look, three weeks, it's still going strong, and then three months later, it's still going strong."

ARE YOU THINKING OF A SPECIFIC EXAMPLE WHEN YOU SAY THIS?

I'm thinking about how Union Square Ventures invests in networks. Tumblr, Kickstarter, Etsy, and Twitter were this way. These products are a function of direct decisions that the founders made, plus the audience. The users have come in and are just as much a part of the product as the people who created it are. Twitter is the best example of this. The at-reply, retweet, and hashtag weren't things that the creators made. They were emergent behaviors, and the community invented those conventions. Only after they had taken hold, did the company productize them. There is a relationship that you have to have. You are the shepherd of this thing, but you aren't the engineer. The founders are shepherds. Certain principles probably guided them to make the things that they made, but they actually don't know where it's going either. They are the closest to understanding the thing they can't quite articulate, which is not functionality oriented. The founders aren't functional or rational. If you are in charge of the product, the product has to be founded on principles you believe in. Maybe you have a debate about the principles, but you have to have a sense of what they are; things then adhere to that.

Tumblr is not a blogging platform. It's a personal place for self-expression. It just happens to resemble what you and I *call* a blogging platform, because that's the dominant model by which we express ourselves on the web and in social functions. If I were to look at it from a functional perspective, I would have built comments and followers. But when David Karp built Tumblr, he didn't want people to feel bad. If you are building a positive place for self-expression, you don't want people to feel bad.

If you launch a blog, and you only have one or two followers, why would you want to publicly advertise that? It'll make you look like you have no friends. But you can have a great experience on Tumblr if you only have a few friends, because you aren't exposed. With comments, like we see on YouTube, there's a cesspool for hate, racism, and all sorts of negative stuff. People are crapping on your page. So if I want to say something negative about you on Tumblr, I have to reblog your entire post and add my nasty little comment; then it's only seen by people following *me*, not by people who are following *you*. Two or three years ago, I would have looked at that complexity and said that was an overcomplicated, convoluted, unusable system that was poorly thought through and hacked together. Now I see that these decisions are actually very elegant and are rooted in how you want people to feel. My mentality before was "no database table left behind." You have a field in the database, so you have to build a feature around it, otherwise, kittens are dying. [laughs] I thought very functionally about building a social system. But it really should come from a sense of feeling.

This gets back to the culture. Let's say that I was enlightened enough to see this back in 2004. I couldn't have pulled it off as a product manager because so much of the culture of the West Coast was engineering oriented. That is what that region is known for. The dominant model of thinking through a social system was through a functionally oriented lens. And Karp, from Tumblr, isn't a product manager; he's the founder of the company. He is able to back that into the fundamental principles of the organization. If you can't see the world that way, you'll have a hard time operating in that company.

Compare Tumblr to WordPress, which most people compare Tumblr to because they think it's a blogging platform. WordPress *is* a blogging platform. Its subtlety is in the experience of the developer. That's where the product came about. The methods by which you use plug-ins or themes or contribute a patch to WordPress are all well thought out. The community in WordPress is on the developer side, not on the audience side. In Tumblr, the network is in the audience. If you do a root cause analysis on why that is, it's because Matt Mullenweg is very tied into the development community that built WordPress. That's why the product evolved the way it did. But Karp was focused in different communities, and that's why that invention evolved the way it did. Mullenweg is just as much the shepherd of that community as Karp is of his community. That word, *shepherd,* is how I would describe the role of product management; that can sit anywhere in the organization and has implications based on where it sits, too.

THE WORDS YOU ARE USING ARE EMOTIVE, FUZZY, AND SUBJECTIVE. CAN YOU COMPARE YOUR RECENT EXPERIENCES, WHICH HAVE POSITIONED YOUR THINKING IN THIS MORE QUALITATIVE MANNER, WITH YOUR EXPERIENCES AT CISCO, A LARGE, CONSERVATIVE COMPANY?

It's hard to say. I can't generalize and say, "Because I worked at Cisco, product management at a large company feels like this." I remember a story about how successful products come from everyone on the team knowing what you are doing and why you are doing it. You could ask a random engineer how the feature fits into the larger story.

ISN'T THAT THE NASA STORY? YOU COULD ASK THE JANITOR, AND HE WOULD SAY, "WE'RE PUTTING A MAN ON THE MOON."

Yeah, that's right. That gets exponentially harder when you surround the team with more people. That's why a two- or three-person start-up can navigate its way around a large corporation; it's easier to have everyone on the same page. Everyone, on every day, is making decisions that subtly affect the direction you are going in, and with Cisco, the challenge was that you had a team, and that team had another team around it, and that sat within a business unit, and that was influenced by the other business units; there were so many forces at play that it was very hard to maintain focus. It was hard for everyone to know what they were doing and why they were doing it.

In that model, there's very little room to accidentally succeed. Everything had to be rationally thought out and executed, because that's what large hierarchies do. That's an industrialized manner of making things. But so much of the good stuff that happens comes from people screwing up, discovering, exploring. A failure makes you think of something you have never thought of before. You need room for that. That's what start-ups are conducive for—they allow that to happen. In a large company, there are so many expectations.

You have too many external forces that don't naturally allow for those things to happen.

THE CONVERSATION WE'RE HAVING ABOUT EMOTION AND INTUITION SEEMS AS IF IT'S AT ODDS WITH A CONVERSATION OF HIERARCHIES AND FEATURES.

It's highly specific to a certain kind of invention. If you are making a television, maybe these things don't apply. Or maybe they apply in a different way. But, if you are building for human beings who are social, you have to be thinking about what it means. It's what makes you human.

RIGHT, BUT WE'RE TALKING ABOUT SOFTWARE. IT'S AMORPHOUS. IT'S BITS AND BYTES.

But we're talking about the *application* of software. If you are going to build software for routers and switches, you can make assumptions that you can't make when you build software for human beings. Also, if you are making software just for me—like a to-do list or some sort of utility—you can make different assumptions than if you are building software to connect two people together.

The software part is not the part to focus on. That mistake is constantly made. We assume that how you build software in one case applies across time and industry. Back in 1998 and 1999, people were giving talks at conferences about how it's important to think about the users. That's because, in site after site, app after app, the experiences were horrible. We aren't talking about that anymore, because everyone knows that users are important. Everyone knows you have to consider them during design. People have heard of this field of usability. Professionals who are building products today were kids when the adults were building crappy products for them, and they knew that this was bad.

Now, it's evolved from knowing that users are important to saying, "Hey, you should really consider how people *feel*." Etsy is one of Union Square Ventures' portfolio companies; last year it did something that was fascinating. It became a certified B Corporation. The concept of a benefit corporation is that it allows you to make a change to your articles of incorporation so you can consider not just the shareholders in the decisions you make, but also the stakeholders. Previously, if you didn't make that change, and I make a great offer to buy Etsy completely as a director, you have to consider that offer. If you reject it based on grounds that aren't financially related, you open yourself up to the potential for a lawsuit.

This idea that you can consider the stakeholders comes from Etsy's belief that the value of a network is related to the value of the individuals within that network. Its interests as a company are aligned with the interests of the users. That's an evolution from ten or fifteen years ago, when only users were important.

IT IS AN EVOLUTION, BUT AT THE SAME TIME, IT'S RARE: YOU DON'T HEAR A LOT ABOUT COMPANIES DOING WHAT YOU JUST DESCRIBED. I WONDER IF IT'S POSSIBLE TO TEACH SOMEONE.

Can we teach someone to care? That's much more a function of how someone was raised. What their values are. What their beliefs are. I've often heard of the definition of product manager as "the champion of the user." That's a common definition. But it suggests that there are anti-champions of users. It's like Batman. Batman wouldn't exist without villains; they need each other. It's a very dystopian view of how we should make things. Why can't we all be enlightened?

More and more, I see that the organizational structure has to reflect upon the people. It sounds like a very simple statement, but what it means is that the structures don't all have to look alike. They are like snowflakes.

PRODUCT MANAGEMENT STRUCTURES ARE LIKE SNOWFLAKES?

Right.

THIS ALL SEEMS VERY UNSTRUCTURED AND HIGHLY INTUITIVE. WE DON'T NEED CONTAINERS OR RULES, AND EVERYONE DOES IT DIFFERENTLY. BUT IF THERE ARE NO TITLES OR RULES OR JOB DESCRIPTIONS, HOW DOES ANY WORK GET DONE?

Your question is, basically, what does everyone do every day? The more bodies you throw at something, the more friction you have. The more friction, the more you have to do to get rid of it. If you want to set up a service on the web to serve millions of people, there are frameworks to use, services in the cloud to host your data and to load balance requests. You don't need a team of five people to manage that process. You just need one person. But as much as technology has evolved, interpersonal issues have not. The same HR issues that existed fifteen years ago, with founders not getting along, product and engineering not getting along, junior people not learning fast enough, the organization not set up to foster interns, when you hire marketing, how it communicates about the product when people don't really know what's coming out, bugs not getting fixed—none of that stuff has changed in fifteen years. Those are all still issues. The people issues have not changed. That's at the heart of product management: to reduce the friction between the people and make sure everyone is moving in the same direction.

SO WHAT DO YOU TELL A TWENTY-TWO-YEAR-OLD WHO WANTS TO GET INTO PRODUCT AND WANTS TO ACQUIRE SOME SPECIFIC SKILLS?

When I got into product, I was excited about how the components came together. A lot of my teammates were excited about building individual things, but I was excited about seeing the pieces come together. There are times when you do things that you wouldn't have anticipated. There were times when I was checking in code, because we were short-handed on a release. There were times when I went and bought servers, because we needed someone to do it. You fill a lot of holes for the sake of the team making forward process.

A twenty-two-year-old should go make something. That wasn't necessarily an option fifteen years ago. But today, you can learn to code for free online. You can set up a service for free online. You can market the thing you made to people for free online. You can even raise money for free online. So you can go through that experience, and eventually you'll realize, "I don't do this part as good as other people, and I'll find ways to plug them in." If it succeeds, great, you have a business. If it fails, you have a great experience and stories to talk about that make you very marketable to teams that need people like you.

SO IT'S A BOTTOM-UP EDUCATIONAL PACKAGE: TRY BEING IN CHARGE OF THE WHOLE AND SEE WHAT HAPPENS.

But there's nuance. Are you curious enough? Curiosity will let you see the holes in your team and will lead you to your next insight. It's this *what if* or *what does the data show*. When I was at Tribe, a database administrator basically gave me the keys to the kingdom. She set up a live, replicating version of the production database, partially because I was screwing up too many of our existing systems. So she gave me my own, and I could write whatever code I wanted against it, prototype features using live data, and go in and do my own research. That curiosity led to my ability to make a case for something and have people check out a new idea. We've spent a lot of time today talking about how a product manager is the supporter on the team, but the other half of it is that you want someone who has the talent and motivation to be curious about the thing you are building. That's just as important.

WHAT ABOUT THE MARKET? HOW DOES THIS CURIOSITY EXTEND OUTSIDE THE COMPANY, TO THE POTENTIAL MARKET FOR WHAT YOU ARE MAKING?

Part of what made me a mediocre product manager was that I didn't come from any of the communities that I was building stuff for. It's funny: the thing that would have made me a better, more effective product manager would have been to be a more active participant in the community I was designing for. I was too far removed from the people I was designing for. When you do that, you make assumptions based on stereotypes, and they are heavily influenced by rhetoric and fads. You aren't coming to something that's truly inspired by the people you are designing for. You have to find ways to know the market. If you stay inside all day, you won't get anywhere. You can call it research, or whatever you want, but if you are trying to build software for other people, you have to do anything and everything to find out what their lives are like and what motivates them; it's going to be completely irrational stuff.

The moment you try to put a rational framework around any of it, it fails because people don't think that way. Especially with social things. Emotions aren't rational constructs. If you sit inside all day, all you do is come up with a rational framework about how the world works, and it won't work out like that.

When I was at Tribe, there was a competitive company in Seoul, Korea, called Cyworld. One in four people were on its platform; I didn't understand it at all. How could it get such high penetration in 2004? The product was strange: it was a virtual home or a virtual apartment, and you would exchange and give virtual goods to people. If you were my friend, and you had an exam coming up and were working hard, I could give you a gift in the form of a virtual couch. If you had spent any time in Seoul, you would understand: it's common for lots of people to live in small spaces. If that's the case, it's perfectly natural that one's aspirations take the form of a vocabulary of space—of these New York–style lofts and places where you can customize space and objects as a form of unique expression.

I only understood *that* after I understood Tumblr. It's self-expression through media that we share, whereas I had only thought about identity and self-expression through a limited lens.

You would have to go to Seoul to understand that, see that people are doing these things, and let go of the assumptions that you bring to the table for your own products. It's really hard to do when you are building stuff. When you build stuff, you are so mentally focused and zeroed in on one thing that you have blinders on.

We should encourage people to explore what they are curious about, even if they don't know what to call it. The internet is so transformational that it's resulting in the creation of new object types. These new object types sometimes look like older things we've seen before, but sometimes they are completely brand-new. Just because we can't label it doesn't mean it isn't valid. A search engine, for example. Go back twenty years: what is a search engine?

BUT THE TEMPTATION, ONCE YOU SEE THAT THE OBJECT EXISTS, IS TO CREATE A LITTLE SPREADSHEET WITH ALL THE FEATURES OF THE OBJECT, SEE A HOLE IN THE MARKET, AND ANALYTICALLY FIND YOUR WAY INTO THE SPACE.

When we are confronted by things that are new, we try to characterize them with the vocabulary that we have. That's one way to try to understand it. The better way to understand a search engine is to try to build a search engine. Because in doing so, there are nuances and things you are confronted with where you can say, "I need to make a design decision here. I have to decide if I show ten results or one result. I have to decide if I can show things that are brand-new or two hours old." All of these considerations go into it. That's the better path: to build the things you yourself are curious about. Because even if you fail, you'll learn something about the process that will lead you to the next thing you make, and the next thing, and the next thing. You take that through a few cycles, and then you have this thing that no one has ever seen before; they can't describe it, and maybe you can't either.

That's the luxury of being alive at this point in time. This wasn't a possibility twenty or thirty years ago.

IT WASN'T TECHNICALLY, AND IT WASN'T CULTURALLY EITHER, BECAUSE EMOTION-BASED DECISIONS WERE THINGS COUNTERCULTURES DID. THEY WEREN'T RESPECTED.

If you were creating a band twenty or thirty years ago, you could make some conscious decisions about what genre it was. That was the way to communicate who you were and get people interested in you. But today, music is so genre-less. It's the combination of so many influences. These aren't conscious decisions. No one wakes up and says, "I'm going to design a band that is 30 percent Cuban funk, 20 percent classical . . ." You are beholden to the thing you make.

WHICH IS AN EXTRAORDINARILY ARTISTIC WAY OF THINKING ABOUT PRODUCT MANAGEMENT AND CREATION.

I've never been more bullish about an MFA degree than I am now, because of what I've seen in the market around accelerators and incubators that are trying to manufacture an outcome. It's not just from companies; it's in educational institutions as well. People understand that a huge change is happening, and they are trying to reorient themselves, trying to fit themselves into a process. But that assumes that what is happening is a rational process, and that's not the case.

product strategy
sketching a playbook of emotional value

Joe is in a good mood. The team has arrived at a great product vision, and he has a list of design constraints and a stack of hand-drawn sketches that support it. The idea is simple. LiveWell's servers will send its users text messages throughout the day, asking them how they are feeling at that moment. They can respond via SMS, typing back a simple score of one to five. Simultaneously, the app will absorb incoming data from linked products like the Nike wristband or Fitbit, status updates from the user on Facebook and Twitter, and his calendar and mail apps. Then, it will mash it all together to produce a daily suggestion for each user: something to know, do, or understand in order to reconcile how he feels during the day with what he is doing during the day. It's concise, it makes sense, and it's supported by the research the team has done. What's more, Joe is convinced there's a large gap in the market for such an app.

Joe is also excited because the company is expanding. He's hiring an interaction designer, and the development organization is ready to bring on another developer. The product is starting to formalize into a clear path forward, and it's time to start building it.

But there's a tiny hint of uncertainty in the back of his mind. Joe remembers an experience he had at his last job. His group had attempted to launch a new product, and Joe had been unable to communicate the feeling of the product to the developers. They had captured the features and capabilities, but the final product was missing a sensibility, a soul. The result had been visibly unsuccessful.

UNDERSTANDING DESIGN STRATEGY

A "design strategy" is a long-term plan that's focused on how best to tame technology. The playbook for your design strategy describes a path toward realizing the value proposition of your products or services. In a business, a design strategy complements and intersects with both a business strategy (what to build, based on market dynamics and competitive expectations; what intellectual property [IP] to leverage; what core competencies to flex), and a technology strategy (architecture, security, platforms, etc.). It's a lens, just like business or technology. The three strategies are really one, because they are inextricably linked.

Josh Norman, previously principal design manager for new business creation at Procter & Gamble, describes the process at P&G: "In a big company like P&G, designers and design managers are principled, accountable, and work strategically and interdependently. They have to think about today, but also must be aware of the long game. They are intuitive and empathetic, but they also have a process they can articulate and use to drive alignment. They actively 'sense' trends and movements and share these with teams and management as contextual examples that can influence thinking and business choices." For Norman, design is a fundamental part of business strategy, not something extraneous. He continued, "When it all clicks, great design simplifies complexity and becomes more than any individual project or product: it becomes a beautiful synthesis that everyone in an organization feels like they already know. Design impacts platforms and product lines, helps to define consumer and technical requirements, establishes brand identity guidelines and design languages, and creates inspiring strategies that live beyond a role or assignment. You know you've done a good job as a design manager when someone else gets an award for your work, presents it back to you, and explains it better than you did."[1]

Many start-ups avoid the idea of formalizing a strategy entirely, probably because they don't have time. When they do have an articulated strategy, it's often buried and scattered across various documents like a pitch deck, a website, and in assorted Word documents. More frequently, it exists in the air as spoken words between a few founders. In larger companies, a strategy is usually articulated at executive levels, but then diluted into small strategic imperatives as it trickles through the company. However, this approach doesn't work in the context of design strategy. A design strategy is *all about details*, so it's critical to map the strategy in a comprehensive and concrete manner.

A design strategy shows the value your products and services will bring to people as a goal, and the broad steps you'll take to achieve this goal. Typically, these broad steps involve technology, and when they do, the focus of a design strategy is on minimizing the seams of that technology or the transition points where people have to interact with the technology. Design strategy is a form of storytelling. These stories show how technology disappears and people experience a positive future.

Imagine that you are a social entrepreneur. Your mission is to eradicate poverty, and your vision is a world without inequality. Your strategy may be to launch, in the next twelve months, a new set of services designed to treat the psychological, physical, social, and spiritual needs of the homeless. A business lens shows how this will be financially sustainable (unfortunately, the business strategy of most nonprofits and NGOs is "acquire grants," which isn't sustainable and requires a huge amount of overhead). A technology lens shows the SMS-delivery architecture that you'll leverage or the rollout of a new web-based platform for case workers. A design lens emphasizes the narrative of use—how the homeless will interact with the services, what types of experiences they'll encounter, and how the service will evolve over time. The design strategy is a set of stories that progresses as your products and services progress, and illustrates the value proposition of the offerings.

In this case, the design strategy might describe how the new peer-to-peer learning platform will empower a homeless person to gain self-esteem, how a new integrated résumé system will present workforce benefits to those reentering the workforce, and how a new SMS-based system can inform a homeless person about sleeping options for the night and communicate the results to case workers. The design strategy describes a path to an end game, emphasizing the value for people.

A design strategy should, like any other strategy, be formalized in an artifact. Put another way, if you don't write it down, there's little chance that anyone will remember it, believe in it, or act on it. And because a strategy is about a future state, it's useful to include means with ends—to show both the road map that will be used to achieve the strategic results as well as the intended strategic goal.

PowerPoint is the go-to medium for the development of most strategy documents, but strategy documents are too important to be relegated to such a conventional, boring medium. For maximum effect, use a really big, floor-to-ceiling timeline of value-based activities. When you print things really big, they come to life. People can't help but notice them. If you hang a thirty-by-fifteen-*foot* road map in the lobby of your building, you can bet that people will notice it and talk about it. They'll absorb the totality of the road map, realizing that strategy is long term and requires patience. There's a sense of practicality to a strategy when it's accompanied by a timeline of actions. It shows both vision and realism at once. (You'll learn about such an example in chapter 6.)

A design strategy takes three artifacts—an emotional value proposition, a concept map, and a product road map—and combines them into a single tool. (You'll learn how to make all these artifacts in the next two chapters.) Keep in mind that a design strategy is more than just a tool or document, because it can act as a powerful reminder of purpose. A good strategy becomes ingrained within the DNA of the company and becomes second nature to the people who need to execute it. Why are we doing the things we're doing? How do they all relate? Why am I in the weeds, sweating the details of this tiny user interface decision? Oh, that's why: because it builds to a much grander, more purposeful intent. A design strategy gives you a reason to go to work.

IDENTIFYING THE EMOTIONAL VALUE PROPOSITION

The first part of the design strategy is the emotional value proposition. A value proposition is a promise to produce value for a customer. The promise is communicated to customers comprehensively; it's both explicit in the value line (and communicated through marketing) and also implicit in the design decisions that define and shape the product (and communicated through product use).

To understand your value proposition, ask—and answer—this *value question*: what can someone do *after* using or acquiring your product that she couldn't do *before* using or acquiring your product?

Value is often described in an economic sense as a form of wealth that's created, such as money, or another scarce resource, time. It's tempting, then, to answer the *value question* from a standpoint of utility, describing the practical things your product helps someone do. For example, if you were just starting a search engine to compete with Google, you might describe how your product "helps people find information." That makes sense; it's even part of Google's mission statement, "to organize the world's information and make it universally accessible and useful." Its little publicized value line, Search, Ads, and Apps, echoes this.[2]

Google's value statement is about getting things done and increasing efficiency. It is clear, straightforward, and can easily be tracked and measured. You can use a statement of value as vetting criteria for new features and functions, or even for the organization of the company. When someone has a great idea for a new product, you could ask, "How will this new idea support our value line of search, ads, and apps? How will it help people find information? How will it help organize the world's information?"

But these comments of *utilitarian value* are only a part of the story. A customer will buy or use a specific product not just because of what it *does*, but also because of how it makes him *feel*. To begin to understand the emotional connection between a product and a person, think about feelings, aspirations, desires, and dreams. Ask this revised question: what can someone *feel* after using or acquiring your product that he couldn't *feel* before using or acquiring your product?

Joe's value proposition is stated like this:

After using LiveWell, people can better track the way they feel throughout the day and connect those feelings to events or activities in their lives.

Joe's emotional value proposition is stated like this:

After using LiveWell, people will feel more connected with their body rhythms and will feel more in control of their mental health.

DEVELOPING A PRODUCT STANCE

The second piece of your design strategy comes from determining the product stance. This highly subjective quality common in digital products floats between brand and utility. Product stance is the attitude your product takes, its personality. Stance is manufactured and designed, and from a particular product stance flow features, functions, language, imagery, and other formal design qualities. Stance is similar to, but different from, market fit, usability, or usefulness. Stance can be applied purposefully or haphazardly. It can evolve from an existing brand language, or it can be created from scratch. Product stance can evolve from an understanding of users, from an understanding of market, or from the attitude and approach of an individual designer. Product stance is about feelings.

But feelings are hard to formalize and hard to quantify. Conversations about feelings in analytical environments (like businesses) are hard to find. Even if these conversations occur, people find them difficult to have and to understand because the content is highly subjective and the output of the discussion is vague. If the team members decide that they want people to feel happy after using a particular product, they have difficulty translating that immediately into actionable capabilities or activities. Instead of thinking directly about emotions, develop a product stance by thinking about your product as a person. If your product were alive, what kind of person would it be? What attitude would it have when confronted in an anxious situation? How would it respond to a threat? What would your product be in a meeting: Would it be creative or analytical? Would it lead the meeting or sit in the back, doodling? Try to bring the product to life by imagining it having its own personality.

Your product obviously isn't a living being, but when a person engages with it, she'll naturally go through a process that's called anthropomorphism. She'll assign human characteristics to your decidedly not human product. Most simplistically, if your app crashes, she'll swear at it and tell it to go to hell. The process of anthropomorphism can lead to more complicated product relationships that build over time. When you try to understand the stance you want a product to take, you naturally begin to consider time-based interactions, and you frame the relationship between a person and your product as a *dialogue* rather than a *monologue*.

Once you've gotten comfortable with the idea that your product might have a stance, you can start to describe what that stance should be. First, identify the *aspirational emotional traits* you would like your product to present to the world. There are lots of ways to identify these traits, and how you go about identifying them will depend heavily on the style and culture of your product team. Is this a team that embraces an analytical, engineering approach to design? Is this a team that looks to the market for guidance? Is this a team of one—you—in which your vision is driving product development? Or, do you have an existing brand that comes loaded with existing attitude? (See table 4-1 for ways to identify existing attitudes.)

Identifying four or five extremely specific traits works well; the more specific they are, the more useful they will be. For example, compare the aspirational emotional traits for a Lexus and a Mini Cooper. Lexus is a luxury brand, but "luxury" only gives us a vague emotional feeling. Lexus wants to be *luxurious, sensual, coy, aloof, elegant, smooth, romantic*, and *slightly out of reach*. The Mini Cooper, by comparison, exhibits *childlike wonder, carelessness*, and *lightness*; it wants to be *spirited, lighthearted, playful*, and *free*. We know this because we can analyze the cars themselves, the advertisements for the cars, and the purchase experiences. The existing brand language provides clues about the product stance.

Now, use the aspirational emotional traits to establish *emotional requirements*. Like functional requirements, these describe aspects of the product or service that you will build, and like functional requirements,

Table 4-1

Identifying existing attitudes

IF YOU WORK FOR A LARGE, WELL-ESTABLISHED COMPANY . . .	. . . YOUR BRAND LANGUAGE ALREADY EXISTS, AND YOU HAVE AN EXISTING MARKET-BRAND PERCEPTION . . .	. . . AND THIS EXISTING BRAND LANGUAGE WILL DIRECTLY LEAD YOU TO SPECIFIC EMOTIONAL TRAITS THAT MAKE SENSE.
If you work in an engineering culture . . .	. . . the team will expect and respect an analytical approach to process . . .	. . . and you will need to rationalize the aspirational emotional traits you select based on data.
If you work in a marketing-driven culture . . .	. . . the team will look to the competition and overall market landscape . . .	. . . and you will need to visualize opportunistic white space as a way to justify the aspirational emotional traits you select.
If you work in a tiny team . . .	. . . you'll have a lot of freedom to make decisions on your own . . .	. . . and so you'll need to have a strong opinion about the type of emotion you want your product to exude.

you can test to see if these requirements have been fulfilled after a product is complete. These emotional requirements take the form of sentences of fact—"Our product will . . ."—and you can introduce these requirements into the same story, point, or defect-tracking systems you already use. The difference between these emotional requirements and functional requirements, however, is that emotional requirements are omnipresent. They exist across every use case, in every facet of the product, and dictate, describe, and artificially contain every other product, quality, usability, marketing, and design decision that follows. Simply, they trump everything.

Mike Kruzeniski, design lead at Twitter and a former creative director at Microsoft, says these emotional requirements become the "soul" of a product. No matter what gets cut due to timing, budget, or market constraints, these things cannot be eliminated, or you have no product left. When I asked him to explain how he thinks about soul, he described it as a set of minimums:

> Soul is really the minimum combination of three things: what the product does, how it behaves, and its form. The formal, stylistic attributes are what breathe life into the functional parts of the product—but they can't exist on their own.
>
> As a designer, I ask myself: "What features can I take away and still achieve my goal? What is the minimal amount of animation or movement that can expose a personality in my product? How can I make my product distinct using only a minimal number of aesthetic elements?"
>
> When these minimums are well balanced, a narrative starts to be revealed about how the design team works. The product is no longer just a product; now, it has a story. It tells you what the designers care about most, the way they make decisions, their character, and what they think is important. When you use a product and feel some sense of connection with its maker, that's where I think you start to feel a soul coming through.[3]

Here are some examples of emotional requirements that might follow from the traits described for Lexus:

Our product will always be revered in a crowd.

Our product will be highly tactile, almost erotic.

Our product will always tempt users to do slightly illogical things.

Our product will always let users feel in control, but will always actually be controlling the users.

These statements sound as if the product were a person. They create a sense of identity for an inanimate object. They become the structure of personality. Later, you'll use the emotional requirements as a *set of constraints* to determine product features, pricing decisions, content strategy, launch priorities, and so on.

These requirements become the way you argue for and select product features. Should the product come in high-saturation Day-Glo colors, or—given the above requirements—would a more sensual, rich, subdued color palette make more sense? Should the speedometer stop at a standard setting, or should it go up to something absurd, like 220 mph? Should the sunroof be an option, or should it come as standard equipment?

Additionally, the requirements become ways you argue for and select product interactions and aesthetic details. Manual window cranks don't make any sense in the Lexus, but subtle dimpling, extremely detailed textures, and smooth transitions with recessed details seem just right. Leather? Of course—how could you *not* have leather, given those emotional traits and requirements?

These emotional requirements become the arbiter of arguments, the way product teams move forward. The product comes alive, because it now has personality. It is no longer inanimate; it has opinions about how it should be shaped and formed. Major emotional inconsistencies are just as surprising and difficult to rationalize in a product as they would be if you discovered them in a friend.

Our fictional character Joe has developed these aspirational, emotional traits for his product:

Our product wants to be **supportive, lighthearted, warm, dependable,** *and* **casual**.

He translates these traits into these emotional requirements:

Our product will converse with the user in chatty, natural, conversational language.

Our product will anticipate negative emotional reactions and offer ways to mitigate these reactions.

Our product will help people feel less loneliness and more togetherness.

Our product will always be affirming.

PRODUCT STANCE DEPENDS ON FRAMING AND PLAY

A strong product stance capitalizes on two of the most important qualities of product development: framing and play.

A frame is an active perspective about a situation, person, or product. We frame experiences all the time. This is how we get through life—by actively considering situations that develop around us and by automatically applying our own lens or filter to a given situation. Framing is a part of being human, and while there's a constant demand in Western civilization to be objective, objectivity is probably an unattainable goal, at least in the midst of experiencing something.

Play is the idea of exploration for exploration's sake, examining and considering different results simply to see what happens. Being playful means being exploratory and curious, and having a desire to try things.

When you consider framing and play together in the context of product development, you arrive at a place of opportunity—*opportunity to reframe a situation from a new perspective, just to see what happens.* When you assign that new frame to your product, you ask it to act in a certain manner, as if it has a somewhat autonomous personality. If the personality has consistency, and the emotional richness of the stance seems credible, the user will experience a rich interaction with your product. And if the user experiences a product stance with resonance, the aspirational emotional traits will actually transfer to the user. A playful, provocative, unexpected frame will resonate with a user who wishes to be playful, provocative, and unexpected. Said another way, a user will *become* more playful, provocative, and unexpected by using the product with this stance.

I have used a nondigital product—a vehicle—as an example on purpose. The aesthetics of a car are obvious, so the personality decisions are overt and obvious. A digital product is much more subtle, but the opportunities for this stance to have a lasting and deep impact are often amplified by the scale and reach of digital output.

Several years ago, Burger King teamed up with advertising agency Crispin Porter + Bogusky to create the "Whopper Sacrifice," a campaign in which users of Facebook were asked to sacrifice their friends in exchange for free hamburgers. If you sacrificed a friend—say, Joe—the message would show up on your Facebook wall that you thought a free hamburger was worth more than your friendship with Joe. As much as Whopper Sacrifice was a product, the product exhibited a highly irreverent product stance. That irreverence transferred to the hundreds of thousands of users who elected to sacrifice friends for burgers. That was a product decision purposely to enhance an emotional value proposition and design strategy.

Matt Walsh, executive vice president at Crispin Porter + Bogusky, who was in charge of the campaign, explains that the idea of this irreverent tension is "the foundation on which all of our brand ideas are developed. We find that the equities and truths inherent in our clients' brands are often contrary to a cultural perception or temporary trend. Their product truths conflict with what people have come to understand as real and true. This creates tension that we can exploit. If we frame that product truth in a way that's at odds with cultural convention, we create tension and potential energy that is eventually released in the form of cultural conversations and reappraisal of products, categories, and the world around us."[4]

MailChimp, a tool for sending mass mail to a mailing list, acts as a playful friend with a whimsical sense of humor. When you preview your mail, if you stretch the screen too large, the monkey's arms fall off.[5] That was a product decision made purposely to enhance a product stance. MailChimp's CEO Ben Chestnut explains that these decisions were initially made to "advertise the company as an attractive workplace for creative programmers and designers."[6] Aarron Walter, director of user experience at MailChimp, explains that Chestnut was "coming up with funny ways to show people how wide their e-mail could be, and they thought of those carnival ride signs that show you, 'You must be this tall to ride.' Because the preview is shown in a pop-up window, which is resizable, they thought it'd be funny if Freddie's arm just kept extending with the window. But at a certain point, it just looked absurd. His arm couldn't stretch that far!"[7]

In both examples, nonutilitarian functionality has been added or manipulated for the single purpose of supporting a product stance through emotional appeal. This appeal might take the form of a story, an animation, or a joke.

CONSIDERING ANALOGOUS SITUATIONS

A third part of your design strategy, along with the emotional value proposition and product stance, is an understanding of analogous emotional experiences.

First, think about the *insights* and *goals* you've identified through your research. If you are working in the space of medicine, you might have described insights such as, "People want to stay healthy with minimal effort" or "People don't understand or trust scientific terms for medical conditions." You might have identified goals such as "Safely treat a disease" or "Understand treatment plans." Author Alan Cooper observes, "When technology changes, tasks usually change, but goals remain constant," so these high-level goals will be true irrespective of the medium of your solution.[8]

Based on your insights, describe the uniquely human interactions and emotions that are typical when people try to achieve the goals you've identified.

Some interactions and emotions that support the goal of "safely treat a disease" include:

- Remember to take a pill each day.
- Feel confident of progress being made.
- Check in with a health professional occasionally.

Some interactions and emotions that support the goal of *understand treatment plans* include:

- Read about the treatment plan in plain language.
- Discuss complexities with other people.
- Feel in control.

Next, think about a comparable and analogous situation that has nothing to do with health care. In what other situations are all of these qualities true?

- Remember to [do something] each day.
- Feel confident of progress being made.
- Check in with a professional occasionally.
- Read about [the situation] in plain language.
- Discuss complexities with other people.
- Feel in control.

There's an analogue in many situations—from things like gardening to enrolling in an executive MBA program or training for a marathon. All these situations require daily interactions, have a long and slow sense of progress, require infrequent but regular professional interactions, have lots of jargon that can be described in plain language, and require a feeling of control.

Take one of them—say, training for a marathon—and begin to describe how the process happens over time. Sketch a timeline of it and describe the main artifacts that support people as they train. For example, people wear *devices* to track their progress throughout the day. *Calendars* help coaches prepare and remind people of their training regimen. People attend *groups* in order to receive encouragement and help. And people read *magazines* with inspirational stories about people just like them succeeding.

All these artifacts become prompts for your brand-new product in health care, offering touch points for potential features for your new product. Ponder the calendar idea, the group idea, the magazines, and the devices, and think about why these are so effective in the analogous situation. Then steal the ideas liberally and repurpose them in the new context. This method of *looking at similar situations* works because of your brain's ability to use analogy across patterns. According to cognitive scientist Douglas Hofstadter, analogy is at the core of all human thinking and is the connective tissue that helps us make sense of the world around us.[9] In order to leverage rich analogies, you'll need to have a rich worldview—one in which it occurs to you to think of marathon training or gardening. So, in addition to this technique as a prompt for sparking momentum, consider how you can more generally broaden your view of culture and society. That might mean reading new blogs that have nothing to do with software, start-ups, or products, and going to conferences that are two or three times removed from your comfort zone.

In this chapter, you learned how to build and structure an emotional value proposition in order to drive a product vision that focuses on emotions, rather than utility. You also learned how to develop a product stance, giving a product a particular voice, and how to leverage analogous situations to make experiential leaps. In the next chapter, you'll learn how to fill in the details of that strategic vision with product details, so your product can come alive with character.

- -

AN INTERVIEW WITH MARK PHILLIP,
ON RESTRAINT IN PRODUCT DECISIONS

- -

Mark Phillip is the CEO of Are You Watching This?!, a sports excitement analytics company based in Austin, Texas. RUWT?! uses algorithms to identify exciting sporting events in real time, whether it's a no-hitter in baseball, penalty kicks in soccer, or a super over in T20 cricket. The B2B company licenses the data to sports and media companies worldwide to power mobile applications, digital billboards, or the lights on the roof of a skyscraper.

A Brooklyn-born, MIT dropout, Phillip is obsessed with exploiting technology to unleash people from their devices. Before founding RUWT?!, Phillip split his career between enterprise software consulting and advertising, working with large brands such as Best Buy, Boeing, Chase, Ford of Europe, John Deere, Lands' End, and Toyota.

- -

MARK, TELL ME ABOUT YOU AND YOUR COMPANY.

Are You Watching This?! gives you a digital tap on the shoulder when it's time to run to the couch: we search for exciting sporting events and notify you so you can watch before it's too late. We power big companies like Fox, CBS, and Telstra. When there's an exciting game happening, they can do anything from send a push notification in an app, trigger a DVR auto recording, or send a message to a massive billboard flashing "UPSET!" on the side of the road.

At the core of our application is our excitement rating. We have a numeric value that starts at zero and goes to infinity. Zero is the most boring game possible. Once you get to around three hundred or so, you get into pretty special games. We have four levels that layer on top of the numeric values. Epic starts at 275. Epic is a no-hitter in the bottom of the eighth inning. It's what is going to be the conversation at work the next day.

So the number goes up and down; that's the core of what we sell. It enables things that are really big. It enables DVR recordings, billboards, and other massive public events. For example, we took over a hotel with a light that corresponded to the status of a game. It was like a big bat signal for sports fans.

I've been doing this, essentially by myself, for seven years and two months. There have been a few contractors here and there, but it's my baby and my vision. I have one major competitor called Thuuz; the difference between us is interesting. Thuuz has fifteen employees and $5 million in funding. I'm a one-man shop, funded by credit cards. Actually, this is a profitable year. My credit card score went up 115 points this year, compared to a few years ago when it was 0. In ten years, there will be a great MBA case study comparing Are You Watching This?! to Thuuz. It's first mover versus second mover; B2B versus B2C. A lot of the decisions I considered making are being made by Thuuz with funding, which I decided to stay away from. Thuuz is a parallel universe company doing what I do, but doing it very differently. It's interesting to watch a lot of the decisions that I sometimes second-guess being made by a totally different company.

SO, IN MANY WAYS, YOU ARE LIVING THE INTERNET DREAM—THE LONE FOUNDER, BLAZING A TRAIL BY YOURSELF. WHAT'S IT LIKE TO GO IT ALONE?

The blessing and the curse is that I have complete control over the vision of the company, but I have no one checking up on me. So sometimes I make pretty obvious mistakes. The biggest mistake I've made so far is not attacking iOS when it first came out. Before Apple had an App Store, it had a Web Store, where it published web apps. Are You Watching This?! was one of its first featured sports apps. But when Objective-C was introduced and you could build native apps, I never got into it. I had to buy a Mac, and I was broke at the time, and I didn't want to learn a whole new language. If I had had someone who had said, "Don't be an idiot—this is important to check out," things would be very different.

A big part of my decision making is about what I'm going to spend my time on; I spend a lot of time on my algorithm. In a basketball game, it's exciting if the game is tied, and a little less exciting if it's down by two, and a little less exciting if it's down by four. I could have an algorithm that just worked linearly like that. But it turns out that the typical idea that a tie game is most exciting isn't actually accurate. A one-point game is way more interesting than a tie.

So there's always more you can add to an algorithm. It's never finished. A big part of figuring this out is letting it sit in your head, watching games and thinking, "Does this actually make sense?" It takes a while to let things stew. I would love to spend my entire day working on the algorithm and doing what-if scenarios. But I can't. So it always feels as though it's 95 percent done.

So the tough part is, as a one-man shop, how do I split my time between perfecting the craft and selling the product? Many first-stage entrepreneurs wonder, "How good does my app have to be before I can sell it?" Making that "good enough" decision is one thing. But once you get past good enough, that's what I struggle with the most, because it can take infinite time to polish this to perfection. And I can't focus only on one thing, because I have all of these other things to do.

Our customer Telstra, a big Australian telecommunications company, reached out a year ago to say that it wanted to rebrand, and in March, it launched a new brand called SportsFan. So it is using Are You Watching This?! data to rate cricket and rugby. It's been interesting working with Telstra to build a brand-new app for brand-new sports, with brand-new algorithms. For me, there's been a lot of product management to figure out what we're actually building.

Australian sports are extremely different. For example, gambling there is legal and it's everywhere. You walk into a bar, and there's gambling run by the government. It might even be subsidized by the government. So we're building gambling odds into the app. I had to learn to understand that mind-set.

There's a different pace to sports there, too. In the United States, one out of four days of the year has a hundred sporting events. On November 17 of this past year, there were 580 games in one day. But when you go to Australia, there are matches on Friday, Saturday, Sunday, and Monday. Then Tuesday to Thursday, it's entirely quiet. It's less about needing the tap on the shoulder to run to the couch, and it's more about being in "sports mode" on the weekend. Understanding the customer was the toughest thing for me to wrap my head around. But once I did that, I was able to marry the end-user demographic with Telstra's needs and provide value through Are You Watching This?! That's what I see as product management. I don't call it that, though. I call it "the vision"—what will delight users so they keep coming back to the product.

HOW DO YOU ARRIVE AT THAT VISION?

For many people, it's an analytical process. For me, it's gut. People ask me if I did any market research when I first started. I didn't. I'm just building a site

I always wished existed. A lot of people will see a market opportunity and think, "I can make money here. I can build something here, I can do a business plan here, and this looks profitable." You can do great things that way, but after three or four years and it's not successful, it's very easy to lose motivation.

I love what I do. I get to watch sports all day and talk about math. I went 4.5 years without making a single dollar, without a single customer. I was able to move the company away from things I didn't want to do and toward the things I enjoy, minimizing my weakness and playing to my strengths. My vision is driven by gut, because I enjoy sports so much. I could spend the rest of my life just doing sports and technology.

HELP ME UNDERSTAND WHAT YOU MEAN BY "DRIVEN BY GUT."

It's about understanding your audience and learning how to be a translator. One of the reasons I was good at consulting, which I did before this, was because I could translate from geek to English. I got good at identifying that this person has this pain point, and this is how I'm going to sell to them, and technologically, this is how I'm going to solve the problem. It's what makes me enjoy my job, and it's what provides the best stuff of what I do. It's the ability to understand how to teach someone something new, in a way that he is going to get it. It's about what I can enable for people.

Many sports fans miss games. They forget that the Yankees are playing an interleague game against the Cubs and that a channel they never watch is airing the game; they don't put it together in their head. But for those three days of the year, when the Yankees are at Wrigley and it's broadcast on that channel, we want to give you a tap on the shoulder. Sports have the shortest shelf life. You need to watch live. So how can I enable this sports fan to enjoy his sports fandom more? It's not about watching ESPN, and bouncing between ESPN and ESPN2. It's about remembering that NBC Sports is on channel 929, and they are on this crazy tier where their sports don't line up with the other sports channels. It's all of this data, whittled down in a way that allows you to be a super fan, to not be the loser at the watercooler who missed the great game the night before. You have this digital tap on the shoulder, a concierge or a digital buddy who's helping you enjoy sports more.

One of my heroes is Kathy Sierra, a programmer. She has a few quotes that I live with and repeat to myself all the time. One of her best is, "Ask yourself: how do you make your users kick ass every day?"

IT'S A GREAT GOAL, TO "MAKE YOUR USERS KICK ASS EVERY DAY." BUT IT SEEMS SO ABSTRACT. WHAT GENERALIZABLE SKILLS MAKE SOMEONE GOOD AT IT? HOW DO YOU DO IT?

It's empathy. It's about teaching and reading your audience. It's easier for me in the sports space because I love it. If you were a product manager dropped into something you know nothing about, the first and hardest part is figuring out your customer. Who is using it, and why do they hate the current manifestation of it?

It's about figuring out pain points and understanding the customer. Then you have to actually create something. If you do the first two correctly, the last part is easy, except then you have to make sure not to throw in the kitchen sink. You need to give people discrete options, instead of infinite options. Restraint is important as a product manager.

Product managers shouldn't listen to power users. Another Kathy Sierra quote that I love is, "No one is as intellectually curious about your product as you are." People will publicly celebrate the things that work for the diehards. But something like Instagram worked really well, and it's not for diehards. It wasn't a Nikon DSLR that you just spent $3,000 on. The average person who kind of likes photography can suddenly become a badass with Instagram in a few button clicks. He can touch up a few things, and it looks decent or trendy. That's where you get the big value. Even though I'm a B2B company, our product helps the masses. The product that you build has to have a demographic in mind, or else you'll try to please everyone and it just won't work. If you are really looking for mass appeal, it's about focusing on the middle of the bell curve. Imagine the bell curve, where the x-axis is pro-ness or skill. It's how much control the users want. The y-axis is population. When you get to the edges, there aren't a lot of people. But in the middle, if you can paint with a broad brush and make it awesome for those people, you'll be successful.

A product manager has to understand the flow from input to result. Think about cable TV, for example. I would love to redesign it so when you turn on your TV, you don't see an electronic program guide of a thousand channels. Eighty percent of people watch eight channels on their TVs. So don't show me a thousand. Show me the three right now that are going to have the content I love. I never watch ABC Family and I never watch Syfy. But ABC Family plays Harry Potter, and I'll watch that. And Syfy sometimes plays James Bond movies. And I like those. Don't make me hunt for content. Those are product decisions. We often think of design as a drop shadow or rounded corners. But design plays an important part in any of the options that you choose. It's a totally different paradigm or different interaction. You are building something new from scratch, where the basic interaction of channel up, channel up, channel up is totally different from curating and presenting options that are worthwhile.

It's a different expectation. It's Netflix, compared to going to the video store. If you could Netflix everything in your life so that everything understands you, and you *believe* that everything understands you, if the recommendations actually make sense, people will love your product. Compare car dealerships with sites like TrueCar, and Blockbuster with Netflix. Blockbuster is gone. Netflix lives. But car dealerships aren't going anywhere. If you aren't able to educate and curate as well as a human can, the technology is not going to win. It's about building the product that makes the most sense.

Once you have the overarching idea of what to build, you have to get into the heads of people and understand why they hate the status quo. With sports,

I'm used to the mind-set, and I'm passionate about the topic. Product managers are able to do that for things they *aren't* passionate about.

HOW DOES THIS TRANSLATE TO SPECIFIC PRODUCT DECISIONS?

When you come to Are You Watching This?!, you first tell us who your cable provider is, the sports you like, and how good the game has to be before you get alerted. One thing that is conspicuously absent is "How can I filter it for my favorite team." That's a product decision that I made: I wasn't going to build that. It's easy to do, and the architecture can handle it, but I never did it. That decision has crafted the demographic of the site. I want folks who love everything about sports. If it's little league baseball at 2 a.m., they'll get out of bed to watch the game. They won't just focus on their teams. I want generalist sports fans.

Decisions like that—to omit a feature—helped shape the community I ended up with, and without decisions like that, I would have really big anomalies in the algorithm. I saw this early on. I was on a radio talk show in Buffalo in 2007, and our site crashed under the weight after the interview. So many people came to the site, and I wasn't ready for it. Then every time there was a Buffalo Sabers game and a Bills game for months later, it was spiking through the roof. Eventually it faded away, but it was scary, because it broke the algorithm. The omission of the feature—picking your team—actually made the product better and the algorithm better. I love what it does for the community.

IT'S A WEIRD CONTRADICTION: TO SAY YOU ARE GOING TO EMPATHIZE WITH USERS, AND THEREFORE YOU AREN'T GOING TO GIVE THEM WHAT THEY SAY THEY WANT.

Understanding what the users want and what that would lead to is what made me realize I don't want that in the product. Saying no is important, even though you know saying yes would delight a good chunk of users. I had enough vision to realize that it would actually hurt the product. If you ever went to a car salesman and he gave you a twenty-page book about every car on his lot, you would walk out. You would call him lazy. He's making you do all the work. But somehow we are OK with doing that on the web and in apps. There's a bit of bravery for a product manager to say, "We're not doing it like that. We won't give them all the power. We'll whittle it down." It's generally not so easy to do. It's radical.

Restraint is tough, and curating is tough, but if you can do them both together really well, that's where the good stuff happens. Bang for the buck is so key. There's an interesting cadence and rhythm to adding features to an app once you've launched it. It's an art and a science to determining which features you launch when.

WHAT DO YOU TELL SOMEONE WHO WANTS TO DO WHAT YOU DO?

No one's ever said that to me. Whatever you start doing, don't do it by yourself. It lacks perspective. You can't figure out what makes sense and what doesn't. It's easy to go down a rabbit hole, to build something because it's elegant code-wise—and no one will ever use it.

It's important to practice making people talk. One thing I tell developers who don't like networking and feel really shy is to try to charm a customer service rep over the phone. It's totally free, and you can hang up any time you want, but if you can make someone on the phone laugh or get him to talk about his day, it's a win. It's about having the ability to get people to open up.

You have to be able to listen really well. Being able to get someone to come out of his shell is a skill. Don't worry about being exciting. Instead, ask a lot of questions. Be interested, not interesting. When geeks go to an event, they'll just want to talk about this great thing they are building. But instead, ask someone about what he does. If you can get good at asking the right questions, you can tease out the pain points of something. Ask them, "Why are you doing that? What's the problem you are solving?" Because if you can meet someone, hear his pitch, ask him two questions, and then give him an idea that he's never heard before, you are in a really good spot. If you can get better at that, hearing people's pitches, teasing out pain points—no matter how small they might be—if you can create a product on top of that, that's the key to everything you do as a product manager. Understand the problem as quickly as possible, identify the pain points, and build the right solution on top of it.

product vision
crafting the product details

Joe double-clicks an e-mail attachment from his interaction designer. It's a revised concept map of the application that shows the entire product at a glance, but at a high level of detail. As he reviews the map, Joe's mind starts to wander to think about version 2.0, but he quickly shakes his head and brings himself back to reality. They haven't even launched version 1.0, and Joe does his best to avoid getting too far ahead of himself.

He's sure the product is strong. It's small—there are about thirty screens, with two main flows—and it makes sense. It's achievable and doesn't rely on a huge amount of complicated technological infrastructure. But Joe is concerned that the current version doesn't pack in enough functionality to be worthwhile. He's not sure if there's enough "there, there." He looks at the development calendar and starts thinking about how he can bring more functionality to life, faster.

DEFINING THE PRODUCT

Digital products are difficult to think about in their entirety, because their boundaries are invisible. Compare a simple software application to a physical product like a chair. You can look at the chair, walk around it, and judge the size of it; you can form a mental representation of the extremities of the object and commit to memory a fairly strong representation of "chairness." You can even sit in it, giving you a sense of proportion and sturdiness. If it's an older chair, and you've recently replaced the seat, it would look new, and you can map that to your mental model of the object. If you were the product manager for the chair, you could certainly picture the chair in your mind. You could close your eyes and describe all its features, styling, and differentiators.

But there's no way to understand how big a piece of software is by looking at it or using it, and there's no good metric to track its size. Should you count lines of code? Number of screens? Even counting features carries a level of abstraction that's difficult to rationalize. Additionally, many apps include legacy code and new code, but there's often no obvious way to judge if the digital "seat" has been replaced. A savvy user may notice aesthetic changes from screen to screen, but would not notice most inconsistencies. Even more difficult is picturing software in your mind. Try it: close your eyes and think about a simple piece of software. Can you picture it? I don't mean a single screen. Can you flow through the software in your mind's eye as you might imagine walking around a chair?

As a product owner, you need to have an accurate mental model of your product. You need to understand the size, the features, the code, and the visual inconsistencies. Over time, you'll build a large portion of this mental model simply by becoming familiar with the product and using it. Even a small product is elusive and difficult to hold in memory at a given time, so a product map becomes a critical tool for managing the complexity of your product.

In its most simplistic form, the map is a visual abstraction of screens, features, flows, or people. The map helps you understand how a person will use your product to achieve his goals. You can point at a series of steps and make a concrete statement about how a user will move from place to place. Additionally, you can form a definitive understanding of scope, complexity, and consistency. At a glance, you can determine if a particular sequence of steps is consistent, if a user can move from one place to another with ease, and if a set of features is available in the way you expect it to be.

BUILD A PRODUCT CONCEPT MAP

At some point, most professionals find themselves in positions of selling: of persuading a skeptical audience that their vision of the future is a good one and is worth pursuing. Most professionals rely on a verbal, logical argument as if the best argument is the most rational. Whether that *should* be the case is debatable; it certainly isn't the case in most organizations, where stakeholders are often persuaded by their emotions.

When a designer presents his product, a successful argument for a future state is usually made through a combination of emotion and narrative, appealing to the heart and soul. Concept maps are a way of persuading an audience while at the same time educating it, helping the audience to see the world from a new perspective (yours), and giving it a mechanism through which to make sense of your vision.

Step 1: List the nouns and verbs.

A product concept map is a tool for showing relationships between the conceptual sections of your product. Typically, it links nouns with verbs; it connects people or artifacts with processes or action. The first step toward creating a concept map is to identify the nouns and verbs. Think about the words you've previously used to describe the product stance and emotional value proposition, and extract language that describes people, artifacts, systems, processes, actions, and reactions. Write these in two separate lists—a list of verbs, and a list of nouns. Joe's lists might look like those shown in table 5-1.

Table 5-1

Joe's list of nouns and verbs to create a product concept map

NOUNS		VERBS
Mobile phone	Alert	Send
SMS	Body rhythm	Receive
Server	Mental health	Track
Feelings	Emotions	Identify
Chart	Graph	Learn

Step 2: Order the lists based on emotional value.

Critically analyze the lists of nouns and verbs, and start to prioritize the items based on how much value they have or provide to a user. Prioritize the nouns based on what they help people do, accomplish, feel, or think.

Prioritize the verbs based on which actions are most important in driving a valuable and desired outcome.

Joe's list, prioritized, is shown in table 5-2.

Table 5-2

Joe's list of prioritized nouns and verbs

NOUNS	VERBS
Body rhythm	Learn
Mental health	Track
Feelings	Identify
Emotions	Send
Chart	Receive
Graph	
SMS	
Alert	
Server	
Mobile phone	

Step 3: Start to sketch the product concept map by creating a main armature out of nouns and verbs.

Create a sentence that connects the first few nouns with the first few verbs. It's OK to add new words to support the sentence or new verbs to add clarity. Joe's first sentence is: "LiveWell helps people learn about their body rhythms and mental health by giving them an easy way to track their feelings and identify a relationship between their emotions and events in their daily lives."

In chapter 4, Joe had created this emotional value proposition: "After using LiveWell, people will feel more connected with their body rhythms and will feel more in control of their mental health." This is a continuation of that activity—a slightly more nuanced, slightly more specific way of describing what the product will do to help people. Joe used a visual language to move from written sentences to a diagrammatic form, drawing this sentence using circles for the nouns and illustrating their connecting verbs with lines (see figure 5-1).This drawing is the armature for Joe's product concept map, the backbone of the system.

Step 4: Add missing nouns and verbs to the map.

Now, add in the missing words like *SMS, alerts, send, receive*. On the existing diagram, determine where the nouns make the most sense, and append

Figure 5-1

First sketch of LiveWell's product concept map

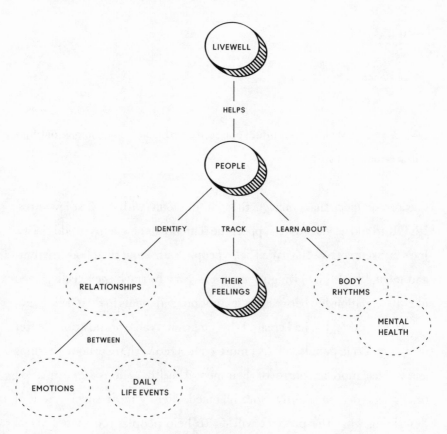

them to the sketch. Again, Joe put nouns in circles and used connector lines to indicate the action-verb relationships (see figure 5-2).

Figure 5-2

Second sketch of LiveWell's product concept map

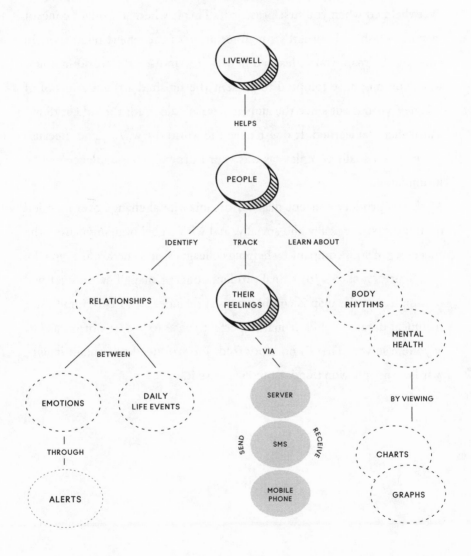

USE THE PRODUCT CONCEPT MAP

Once you've created the map, you can use it internally to build alignment and help others see your vision for the product. It's an extremely effective tool for you because you made it, but the person who has to read it is overwhelmed when you first present it. This is where a product concept map can crash and burn: it's a manifestation of the expert blind spot. In creating the map, you've learned new things and see the world in a new way. You might be tempted to present the finished artifact as proof of this new vision, but since the audience wasn't along for the ride, it didn't learn what you learned. It doesn't see the world the way you do. Because the map is visually complex (as was your learning), your audience will be intimidated.

Use a product concept map for organizational change over a period of months, strategically and socially, and with a goal of manipulating the trajectory of your company by helping colleagues view the world as you do.

Figure 5-3 shows Joe's final product concept map. The product will be simple, but the map is complicated. It includes all sorts of important, technical details. While it makes perfect sense to Joe, it's of no use to anyone else yet. There's no story told. Joe will need to explain it with words or people won't understand it or use it.

Figure 5-3

LiveWell's final product concept map

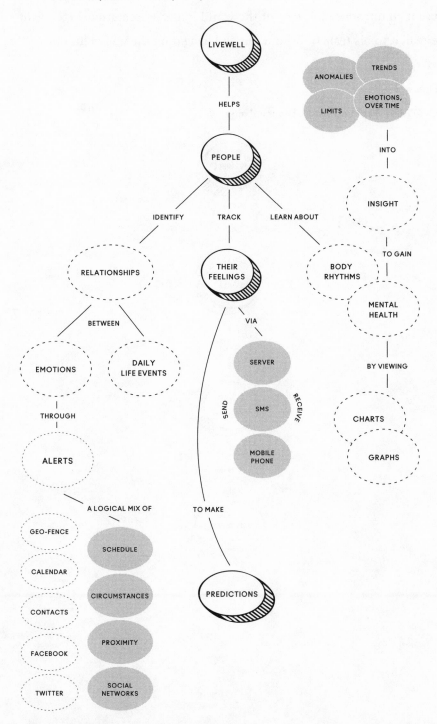

So, Joe might start by introducing a map that looks more like the one in figure 5-4. It seems too simple—just a few major elements—but Joe can use it to introduce his view of the world in his presentations. He might e-mail it to his team or print it out and hang it on the wall in his office.

Figure 5-4

LiveWell's simplified product concept map

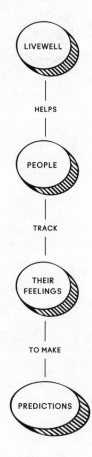

Then, over time, he might replace it with the one shown in figure 5-5.

Figure 5-5

LiveWell's simplified map with additions

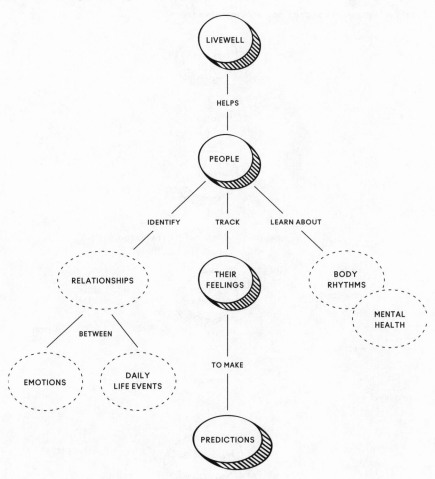

Next, he could describe some of the areas of additional complexity. After a few weeks, he might show the version in figure 5-6.

Figure 5-6

LiveWell's product concept map with more additions

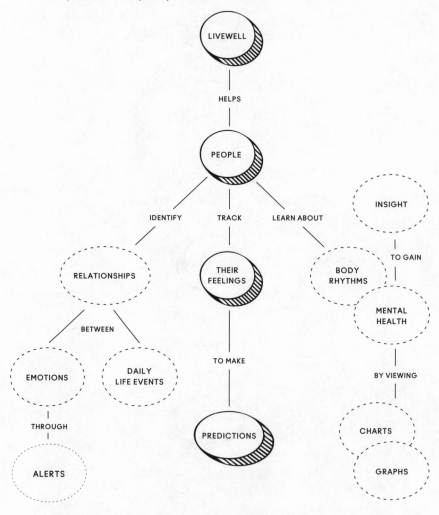

Over time, Joe introduces the map into the organization, and at each step there's no announcement, unveiling, or massive production associated with it. At first, it's not a design artifact in a finished sense. It's released through one-on-one meetings and in presentations and conversations; over time, it gets traction, because it begins to represent something. The diagram itself starts to act as a placeholder for the conversations Joe has had, his vision of the future, and even the roles and responsibilities of individual people or entire business units.

WHAT GOES AROUND COMES AROUND

In a large organization, you can think about a product concept map released in this style as a challenge to the org chart. It's a way of effecting change in a bottom-up fashion, rather than in an autocratic manner. If you use artifacts like this, one day you'll be sitting in a meeting and someone you don't know, from an area of the business you've never had influence in, will present your diagram, in effect, giving it back to you. That's an amazing feeling: your strategic product work has shaped the tenor of the organizational dialogue.

Sometimes, you'll need to introduce the map slowly—taking weeks or even months—until all of the various constituents have accepted it as a common language. Over time, the map will become part of the organizational language. It will become the way people talk about the future. This type of strategic introduction of new design language is extremely powerful. Organizational change can occur through design proxy—slowly, methodically, and purposefully.

Hugh Dubberly, who runs a consultancy in San Francisco, utilizes concept maps regularly in his work to explore new idea spaces. Dubberly explains: "Making a concept map involves clarifying ideas, writing them down, reviewing them, and sharing them with others for their review. In this process, concept maps are tools for thinking, for communicating, and for converging on agreement. A concept map serves as a bridge between two disciplines or two points of view. Concept maps can be useful in the design process whenever designers, clients, and other constituents need to consider more than a simple artifact—when they need to consider contexts, competitors, systems, communities or ecologies, processes, decision trees or goal trees, or other information structures—since concept maps can represent and explain these things."

For Dubberly, concept maps act as ways to understand an idea, but also to share that idea with others: "When designers face wicked problems or complex tangles of issues, creating a concept map can be a good way to develop a common understanding of the situation. Likewise, concept maps can be a good way to summarize an ethnographic study or a series of constituent interviews. Context-setting or structure-defining concept maps can provide guideposts for later steps in the design process and criteria against which to judge later sketches or prototypes."[1]

SKETCH THE HERO FLOWS

At this stage of product development, your product will feel incomplete. You have a sense of the whole, and if you close your eyes, you can kind of "see" the finished product, but the actual product offering is still fleeting. Solidify the product by sketching the main paths through it and actually drawing the interface that a user will see and experience. These paths are called the "hero flows" because they represent how you want a user to move through the system. There are many screens and paths that *aren't* represented in the hero flows, because these ways to experience the product aren't ideal.

Start by creating a list of verb-noun activity pairs, which represent all of the things someone might do with your product. Think all the way through the product life cycle, from when it's purchased to when it's discarded. You might have a list of ten different activities (see table 5-3 for Joe's list).

Table 5-3

Verb-noun activity pairs

VERB	NOUN
Purchase	App
Set up	Product
Create	Account
Establish	Goal
Receive	Text message
Send	Text message
View	Visualization of progress
Upgrade	Account
Discontinue	Account
Retrieve	Password

Now, mark the activity pairs that describe the most common, idealized, and relevant product usage, and name the hero flow that is represented by these items (see table 5-4 for Joe's pairs and hero flows).

Joe has identified two hero flows. The first represents the very first time a user uses his product. It's critical for Joe to nail that, because he's aware that 13 percent of consumers return new electronic devices due to usability frustrations with the software.[2] He wants users to have a glowing first experience, so it needs to be as simple as possible for them to get up and running.

He's also identified a second hero flow that describes everyday use. Joe's product gets better each time a user engages with it, so he wants to

Table 5-4

Activity pairs and hero flows

VERB	NOUN	HERO FLOW NAME
Purchase	App	First-time use
Set up	Product	First-time use
Create	Account	First-time use
Establish	Goal	First-time use
Receive	Text message	First-time use; everyday use
Send	Text message	Everyday use
View	Visualization of progress	Everyday use
Upgrade	Account	
Discontinue	Account	
Retrieve	Password	

make sure he nails the core process of receiving and sending text messages throughout the day, and building a beautiful health visualization that shows progress toward goals.

Now, put on your storytelling hat and quite literally tell a tale of the user, using the product to complete the activities you've listed. Describe the steps a person takes during her activity and assume that nothing fails or breaks. For example, if the user has to log in, tell a story about it happening successfully, not about someone forgetting his password. If the user needs to check out, describe how his credit card is processed successfully, not how he's maxed out his credit limit. Don't worry about the edge cases at this point in the process. Additionally, be pragmatic yet aspirational in your use of technology. Describe situations that may be technically challenging, but not impossible to actually achieve. Floating cars are out, but include things like speech-to-text translation or an aspect equally difficult to implement if it supports your storyline.

First-Time Use

Mary visits the App Store and clicks to install LiveWell Health Tracker. The application downloads, and once it's done, she taps the icon to launch the product. A screen welcomes her and asks her to confirm her first name, which has been sucked in from the phone's OS. It also prompts for her e-mail address. She enters this information and presses Next. The screen tells Mary that LiveWell will prompt her about her health throughout the day and she can set the frequency of these events, but five interactions are recommended per day. A slider lets her quickly change this. She presses Next. The system asks her one last question—to select a goal from a list. The list includes: "Reduce my general anxiety," "Become aware of anxiety-related events in my life," "Gain better awareness of my physical activity," "Learn which people make me angry," and "Learn about my biorhythms." She taps "Become aware of anxiety-related events in my life," and taps "Finished."

The app gives her an indication that she's done and then her phone buzzes. She's received a text message. She taps the alert. It says, "How do you feel right now? Reply back with a number from 1 to 5, where 5 is great!" She taps 4 and presses "Send." The app shows her a big green checkmark and displays a message that says, "We're glad you are having a good day."

Everyday Use

It's 8 p.m., and Mary is sitting on the couch, watching TV. Her phone buzzes with an alert from the LiveWell app. It says, "Got a minute to review your progress?" She taps "Yes."

The screen displays her monthly emotions in a graph, showing two periods that appear to fall below an average. She taps a button labeled "Analyze My

Life," and the app explains to her that her emotions seem to fall every Tuesday around 3 p.m. It also shows that, based on her iOS calendar, she has a meeting every Tuesday from 2 to 3 p.m. with a specific coworker. The one week that the meeting was canceled, her emotions didn't fall. "Interesting . . . ," Mary thinks to herself.

These two hero flows act as bridges between a conceptual product vision and a tactical product definition. As stories, they describe how the product should behave, what functionality it should have, the way people should interact with it, the cadence of interactions, and even the previously defined product stance.

Now that you have written the stories, take the next step to actually visualize the product: draw the hero flows. You don't need to create works of art, and you don't even need to use software to produce these visualizations. Instead, grab a Sharpie and a piece of paper, and use basic geometric shapes and words to show the product interface. Use one piece of paper for each step in the hero flow. (Joe's first-time-use flow might look like that shown in figure 5-7.)

If you think about the hero flows in the context of your concept map, you've started to define both the forest and the trees of the product. The concept map acts as a conceptual guide for how the pieces and parts fit together. The hero flows show how a user moves throughout the system, interacting with those various pieces and parts in order to accomplish a goal. As with the product concept map, sketching hero flows is an iterative process, and you'll go through lots of paper before you get it right. In fact, getting it right may not be the best way to think about your output, which will likely change as you proceed through the process. Instead, treat these flows and the resulting sketches as thinking artifacts. Use them to conceptualize new ideas, to explore different paths, and to consider alternatives.

Figure 5-7

LiveWell's first-time-user hero flow

DEFINE THE VISUAL MOOD

We've explored a number of things that have a direct impact on how a person feels when using your product. Things like the product stance, the emotional value proposition, and even the flow through the system all help shape a certain emotional feel of your product. But the most obvious and rich piece of the emotional design puzzle is the actual aesthetic: the visual mood that's communicated by your product through color, typography, composition, balance, saturation, and imagery. You'll want to engage a visual designer to actually create the product assets, but you can help define the strategic direction of the aesthetic by defining a visual mood. Revisit your product stance and the emotional requirements you identified.

Recall that Joe developed these emotional requirements:

Our product will converse with the user in chatty, natural, conversational language.

Our product will anticipate negative emotional reactions and offer ways to mitigate these reactions.

Our product will help people feel less loneliness and more togetherness.

Our product will always be affirming.

Think about the situations, places, objects, and people that relate to these emotional requirements. Where do people converse in natural, conversational language? Not at church or at city hall; people typically chat casually in their cars, or on their couches, or at the park. Loneliness feels dark, but togetherness feels sunny. Affirmation is about smiling, not frowning. It's about high-fives, not crossed arms. Negative emotional reactions are like rainy days, but positive emotional reactions are like the top of a mountain in the sun. Loneliness is like a cave. Togetherness is hugging.

This type of thinking leans heavily on metaphors and similes. Think about what the emotional qualities are like, where you've seen them, or what they remind you of. Formalize the thinking in a chart (see table 5-5).

Table 5-5

Visualizing emotional qualities

THE VISUAL MOOD I WANT TO EXPERIENCE IS . . .	THE VISUAL MOOD I WANT TO EXPERIENCE IS NOT . . .
Casual conversation in a car, on the couch, or at the park	A formal conversation at a church or a city hall
Sunny togetherness	Dark loneliness
Smiling	Frowning
High-fives	Crossed arms
The top of a mountain, in the sun	Rainy days
Hugging	A cave

Now, abstract these ideas to colors, shapes, textures, materials, emotions, and patterns (see table 5-6).

Table 5-6

Abstractions of emotional qualities

THE VISUAL MOOD I WANT TO EXPERIENCE IS . . .	THE COLORS, SHAPES, TEXTURES, MATERIALS, EMOTIONS, AND PATTERNS THIS REMINDS ME OF ARE . . .
Casual conversation in a car, on the couch, or at the park	Subdued, cloth, simple
Sunny togetherness	Yellow, warm, saturated, skin-toned, earth-toned, smooth
Smiling	Warm, direct, engaging, organic
High-fives	Skin-toned, connective, joining together
The top of a mountain, in the sun	Green, expansive, spotlight, powerful, definitive
Hugging	Joining together, warm, embraced, skin-toned

Now, develop visual boards that show the visual mood by describing the colors, shapes, textures, materials, emotions, and patterns you've identified. Go online and find images that match these characteristics and print them out. Grab magazines and cut out images that make you feel the way these ideas feel. Assemble physical boards that show all of the qualities and try to homogenize the elements.

Your visual designer will use these mood boards to develop her initial visual language for your product. Joannie Wu, a visual designer at frog design, described how she uses mood boards in her process to clarify fuzzy conversations about aesthetics and emotions: "I believe as designers we take for granted how visually sensitive we are. We can often picture the same image in our heads as we verbally describe something in conversation. Unfortunately, this is not the case with most people. The power of mood boarding is to externalize that conversation outside of our heads into something real and definitive, which decreases ambiguity. They are simply a tool to accelerate conversation between two or more individuals." For Wu, the mood board sets a thematic tone so that further conversation can be aligned: "A good mood board always starts with key words or adjectives that verbally define what you are seeing, visually."[3]

EXPLORING, THROUGH ITERATION AND VARIATION

Two of the most basic principles of design process are iteration and variation. They aren't the same, but they are related. *Iteration* is making informed changes to an existing design. These changes may be provoked by user testing or critique. Commonly, these changes are provoked simply through the act of making the previous iteration. This pursuit of perfection can be endless (which drives some project managers crazy). When designing software or services, a designer gains a sweeping sense of design ideas, but typically can't keep all of the details of that sense in her head at once. Iteration is the process that allows her to infuse this sense into the work and overcome the limitations of her own memory. The first pass is a broad stroke intended to get the essence of the idea. For a service, this typically includes a view of the touch points, the people involved, the handoffs, and a few key details. In software, this is typically the hero path I described earlier: the main path a user takes through the interface in order to achieve his single primary goal. The *input* for creating this broad stroke is imagination, and the bottleneck is the ability to remember the various constraints on the design.

Once this broad stroke has been created (drawn, wireframed, coded, and so on), further iterations assume the basic framework as fact. The initial iteration acts as a constraint and becomes rigid. It's OK to refine details and extremities, or review and change aspects of the idea, but the idea itself has been solidified. That's good, because it serves as a creative anchor. It's bad, because you'll now have a sense of ownership of it, and you'll become unwilling to let it go, *even when a better idea presents itself*. Each further iteration serves to solidify details, and the details become taken for granted. In a way, they become facts, and it's difficult to envision the product without them.

Variation is a way of adding a sense of objectivity to design exploration. Variation is an exploration of alternatives. Where an iteration moves an idea forward (or backward), a variation moves an idea left or right, and is not productive in a typical engineering sense because the expectation is that all of the variations (except one) will be rejected. But variations act as provocations for what-if scenarios. Try the A-B-C-Q approach to variation. This is the idea of creating several expected variants, changing minor details (A leads to B, B leads to C), and then creating a wild or surprising jump (Q). These later Q jumps ignore or purposefully reject constraints, established precedent, or social norms; from these Q jumps, risky but exciting innovations emerge.

F. Scott Fitzgerald said that "the test of a first-rate intelligence is the ability to hold two opposed ideas in the mind at the same time, and still retain the ability to function."[4] While many people find it hard to hold opposing ideas in their minds, they find it easier to visualize them on paper or in code, and process them at once after the fact.

Developers are starting to embrace iteration through methods like Agile, a process introduced into software engineering in the early years of web development. These methods are useful, because they treat designed (and developed) artifacts as less precious and more malleable. They are also useful for introducing variation into a development process in order to explore multiple ways of solving a given problem. Allocating development cycles to the exploration of both iteration and variation is extremely beneficial. It's not a waste of time. It's how design works.

RECRUITING PEOPLE TO THE PRODUCT VISION

David Merkoski is a design partner at Greenstart, a venture design studio in San Francisco. When he was executive creative director at frog design, he led a multiyear project for a *Fortune* 50 telecom company that attempted to change the way it built and shipped new products and services. I was on his team; we came up with an artifact that was a massive poster—nearly thirty feet wide by fifteen feet high—that showed the progression from point solutions (and corresponding company silos) to service-based "better together" architecture. We presented the poster to the executives at the client site, where it remained in the lobby of their office. People couldn't help but run into it on their way to work.

I asked Merkoski why he chose this mechanism—this giant, semi-permanent poster—for presenting the product strategy and vision rather than a more typical medium like PowerPoint or e-mail. He said, "Words give things power, but visual models give them form. Models are the essence of visual communication because they become a central artifact that all participants in a design process can point to and rally around; everyone can build a concrete understanding of the abstract and complex ideas being discussed."[5] For him, this giant poster was a model of a complex business strategy, and by hanging it in a public place, he could recruit people to that strategic vision without needing to speak with every person who walked by. The poster was a rich proxy for the complex thinking that went into the development of the strategy itself.

What Merkoski describes—getting people to rally around your product vision—is the most important part of the entire process described so far. You've now seen how to develop a concept map, a set of hero flows, and mood boards that represent the visual mood of your product. You can share these representations of the vision with your colleagues and stakeholders in order to help them build the understanding that you desire.

Print the artifacts and place them in a really obvious and central location in your office, like the lobby or the break room. Make sure every person in the company sees them, understands them, and gets a chance to ask questions about them. Then, set up formal meetings or informally drop in on people and walk them through the vision. Make changes on the fly, using a Sharpie, to capture new ideas you hear from your coworkers, and let them see you make those changes in front of them.

Find ways to integrate the artifacts into meetings, presentations, and e-mails. The more people see these tools, the more they will treat them as the fundamental ways in which to make and communicate product decisions. When you have conversations with people, base them on an artifact; use one of the artifacts to guide the conversation and refer back to it throughout meetings or discussions. Provide the source files to people and encourage them to use the artifacts in their own work. More importantly, encourage them to change the contents to suit their needs.

When you hear of companies being aligned or marching in lockstep, this is what is meant and this is how it's achieved. You need to actively disseminate your product vision and recruit people to that vision. They need to champion the idea, and to do that, they need to feel as though they were a part of its genesis.

- -

AN INTERVIEW WITH FRANK LYMAN,
ON THE CAREER OF PRODUCT MANAGEMENT

In his role as MyEdu's chief product officer, Frank Lyman leads MyEdu's integrated approach to product management, design, engineering, and marketing. Lyman is an experienced educational technology executive and thought leader who has been leading innovation in higher education for over twenty years. While at John Wiley & Sons, Lyman helped create the groundbreaking interactive platform WileyPLUS, now used by millions of students worldwide. Lyman was also one of the founding executives of CourseSmart, the leading e-textbook platform. In addition to his leadership roles at Wiley and CourseSmart, Lyman was chief marketing officer of LibreDigital through that company's successful sale to RR Donnelley, and employee number four and founding vice president of marketing for LifeMinders, which went public in 1999.

Frank Lyman passed away in 2014. He had a massive positive impact in education, and his products have been used by millions of students. He was a great mentor and a kind friend.

- -

FRANK, TELL ME ABOUT YOUR ROLE AT MYEDU.

As chief product officer, I'm responsible for pulling together all of the aspects that go into building our products. That includes research, design, product management, marketing, engineering. It's essentially everything except sales, finance, and operations.

HOW DO YOU THINK ABOUT PRODUCT MANAGEMENT? HOW DO YOU DEFINE IT?

Product management is the function in an organization that pulls together the initiative, the resources necessary to make it successful, and gets it implemented. It's not the place where all of the ideas are generated or where the expertise lives. It's the place that's accountable for advancing the company's goals. A product manager will ask, "How do we take the expertise, what we know and what we learn as an organization, and actually build products and services to advance the company's goals?" This is different for every company. When I was in textbook publishing, a product manager was called an acquisitions editor. At Procter & Gamble, I was an assistant brand manager. It's all product management.

At P&G, my brand team had about four assistant brand managers and a brand manager, and we had overarching objectives for the brand. I worked on the Cheer brand, which at the time was trying to differentiate from the Tide brand, also a P&G brand. We needed to stay at a premium price, but we had to carve out a different value proposition, which was keeping colorful clothes colorful for a longer time. Each of the assistant brand managers had various initiatives that we had to drive, based on what we thought would work for the brand. I was in charge of a revised pricing plan for the main Cheer stock-keeping units, and I had to analyze data from customer research, sales research, packaging research. I had to pull together all of this research, pull together a plan, get support for it, and get it done. Each of the assistant brand managers had initiatives like that.

At the time, I was working with some guys who were working on New Tide. They conjured up Tide with Bleach, which now sells more than Tide, by listening to customers and seeing what was going on in the market competitively. People were using Oxyclean, which was a hydrogen peroxide–based solution that made white clothes whiter. The brand managers pulled together the science, customer feedback, competitive environment, sales feedback, packaging, and branding into an initiative called Tide with Bleach, a billion-dollar brand. That's what good product managers do. They find opportunities and marshal the resources necessary to make them successful.

THAT'S A PRETTY VARIED PATH—FROM DETERGENT TO TEXTBOOK SALES TO EDUCATIONAL SOFTWARE. DID YOU GO TO SCHOOL FOR BRAND MANAGEMENT?

No, no one really does. I was an English major as an undergrad, which is extraordinarily helpful for a product manager, because a lot of the success has to do with being a good communicator. P&G always says it "hires people who can recruit others to a vision." That's a communication challenge. You can have people who are technically very sophisticated, insightful, and competent who don't succeed as product managers because nobody wants to follow them—because they aren't effective communicators or collaborators.

Some MBA programs focus on things like marketing and teach product management and core marketing principles. These programs have a lot of overlap with product management. But I don't know if anyone has a course on product management, or that anyone offers a degree called product management. It has yet to crystallize as an academic function.

WHAT SKILLS WOULD INDICATE TO SOMEONE THAT HE IS GOOD AT THIS THING THAT HE DIDN'T KNOW EXISTED AND CAN'T REALLY STUDY?

One of the more interesting programs is the associate product management program at Google. Google looks for people in the engineering organization who are both insightful and leaders. Then, Google says, "We want you to be an associate product manager, we're going to train you in what that means at Google, and we'll put you in charge of things like Gmail." That product was led by an associate product manager. The better products that Google has created have come out of that program. For each company, it's unique.

At John Wiley & Sons, where I was an acquisitions editor, it was very important to identify salespeople who were capable not just of selling books, but of having a conversation with a professor and convincing him or her to become an author. One of the jobs as a sales rep was to surface professors who should write books. As a sales rep, I was good at that. My father was a professor. I was comfortable with academics; I was comfortable with the strange view of the world that most academics have and engaging in a conversation where I was behaving as a good student. I could build a relationship with them, saying, "You should consider being an author," and telling a story to get an author excited. At Wiley, our product was *academics who can write a textbook.* So people who were good at seeing author opportunities became product managers.

SOME OF THE SKILLS THAT YOU'VE ALLUDED TO INCLUDE LEADERSHIP, VISION, OR CHARISMA. WHAT OTHER SKILLS DO YOU THINK A PRODUCT MANAGER SHOULD HAVE?

Broad credibility. There's an art to being broadly credible. You don't want to come across as "an inch deep and a mile wide," but you want to be able to engage in a conversation with a technical expert in a productive way. Otherwise people will stop coming to you.

Consider the packaging people at consumer products companies like P&G. Packaging is such a precise science; when I was there, I was fascinated by that. P&G was doing its first triple-language product in anticipation of NAFTA, and it wanted to have one SKU in Canada, Mexico, and the United States. How could we get three languages on a single package? The problem was fascinating to me; it's very technical. I was happy to engage in it and was intellectually curious; that gave me broad credibility. The same thing happens here at MyEdu. When I talk to an engineer about moving a certain piece of data from SQL into Mongo, it's not something I know much about, but I'm willing and able to engage at some credible level. That's key for product managers. You can lose an audience if you are uninterested or you just can't keep up. It's hard to be the glue between all of those specialties.

IT SEEMS AS IF THAT BROAD CREDIBILITY IS RELATED TO THE LENS THROUGH WHICH YOU SEE THE WORLD AND BEING INTERESTED IN SHIFTING LENSES TO SEE THE WORLD DIFFERENTLY. CAN A PRODUCT MANAGER START WITH A BETTER OR WORSE LENS?

No. I've seen product managers come from sales, engineering, and QA. Interaction design is a good place to come from. Sales, marketing—you can come to it from almost anything. It's more a function of the company you are at; at Google, an engineering culture, you are probably better off if you come from engineering. Prentice Hall, where I started my career is a sales-oriented company, so you are better off with credibility in sales.

WHAT ABOUT LIBERAL ARTS? AS YOU LOOK AT THE MILLIONS OF COLLEGE STUDENTS SCRATCHING THEIR HEADS AND LOOKING FOR WORK, IS PRODUCT MANAGEMENT A VIABLE DIRECTION FOR THEM?

I can actually see this playing out with one of the social media experts I've hired here at MyEdu. She leveraged her writing skills to get in here, and now she's learning something more applied in the early stages of her career: e-mail marketing and direct marketing. She's also learning what it takes for something to go from an idea to a successfully executed initiative. Ideas are cheap. That's the essence of being a product manager. Ideas are nothing. This isn't R&D. It's just D. You are measured on execution. With a broad liberal arts background, you can find a job where you can go deeper in one place and gain expertise . . . Some liberal arts majors end up becoming technical specialists for the rest of their careers. They could be in something like technical writing, advertising, or creative copywriting. Sometimes people never leave the initial thing that they find they are good at. Sometimes people recognize that they have a broader skill set that is more conducive to something like product management.

WE'VE TALKED ABOUT PRODUCT MANAGEMENT IN GENERAL. CAN YOU TELL ME ABOUT PRODUCT MANAGEMENT, SPECIFICALLY? CAN YOU DESCRIBE SPECIFIC PRODUCT DECISIONS THAT, IN HINDSIGHT, WERE PIVOTAL OR CRITICAL?

When I was at CourseSmart, our biggest product decision was about how to handle mobile. One of the things that makes CourseSmart successful is that it has a broad catalog of titles, because it adopts the lowest common denominator of technology. Every publisher can populate its printed content in the CourseSmart platform without hesitation, because we created something called Page Fidelity. We built an image of the printed page, surfaced with an AJAX layer on top of it. It was like a PDF, but it was dynamic. It had the right level of digital rights management (DRM) that companies were comfortable with. So we had a really scalable platform, with ten thousand textbooks on it. Apple had just launched the iPhone and was hinting at really wanting richer educational content on its platform for future developments. Some of my friends at Apple said, "You guys should really do an app."

But the way our product worked was really challenging on a phone. It was a series of images all stitched together, and when it was shrunk down on the phone, it was hard to read. And we didn't want to move to reflowable text, like the Kindle does, for two reasons. First, textbooks require layout, because you have diagrams and tables. And most importantly, we had DRM considerations.

So the publishers were hesitant to do anything on the iPhone. They were very comfortable with the existing platform and said, "Don't mess with it." But I had a lot of conviction. At the time, Chegg had just spent $6 million acquiring students for Textbook Renter, and I was competing with Textbook Renter. But I didn't have that kind of money to spend. I needed to leverage something novel.

I had a strong feeling that e-textbooks on an iPhone would, if nothing else, be a huge PR success and raise awareness. It would also push us to be more innovative on our platform, which is hard to do when you are a joint venture. I got my colleagues at CourseSmart onboard with my idea; even though it was a little bit risky, we did the song and dance at Apple.

Apple gave us special application programming interfaces (APIs) and early access to the software development kit (SDK), and it helped us do a whole bunch of stuff. Apple connected us with a developer that could do it, because this was the early days in iOS app development. We carved out the budget and created e-textbooks for the iPhone.

We did some student research and realized that students weren't going to read long-form text on an iPhone. What they wanted was to look at one single chart, figure, or graph. They were on their way to take a test and were panning or zooming to that one summary table or chart. That gave us conviction that students really did want this. I knew we would get a lot of complaints like, "No one would read this, it's too small, it doesn't look like Stanza"—which was the ebook iPhone app that was out at the time. But we knew we had the support of students, because they wanted it. So we built it. We got Apple to support the press release, and we talked the *Wall Street Journal* into doing a front-page marketplace exclusive on publishers bringing textbooks to the iPhone.

And it kicked ass. It put CourseSmart on the map. It also pushed us to be more innovative on the technology front, and CourseSmart now has a lead in HTML5 that started with a commitment to being on the iPhone. This wasn't what our board wanted to do, so to get it done, we had to sell to people deeper in our organization and get them behind it. But once we launched it and saw the positive press, people were very supportive.

YOU SAID YOU GAINED CONVICTION AROUND A BIG, BROAD STRATEGIC PRODUCT DECISION—TO EMBRACE MOBILE. HOW DID YOU KNOW IT WAS A GOOD IDEA?

I toggle between my rational brain that says, "Here's what the competition is doing, here's what the data says the customers want," and my emotional feelings that "this will have impact. No one has said they want this, no one has done it before, but I'm looking at it and I think it will have impact." For me, typically, the big idea isn't my idea. It's something someone puts on my desk. I just have a snap reaction that it will have impact. I haven't done any deep analysis of it. Instead, I'm emotionally connected to the idea. And it happens at small scale. I'm emotionally connected to the fact that this functionality should do X, Y, and Z. Some of that comes from having a sense of confidence. While some people are naturally confident, other people are confident because they've done it for a long time. You have to be confident to make those little decisions. You have to be confident in your decision-making process. Rational mind or emotional mind: you have to make the decisions or you won't progress.

A LOT OF THIS IDEA OF "BEING THE GLUE" SEEMS TO BE ABOUT HELPING EVERYONE MOVE FORWARD AND MAKE DECISIONS.

Yes. It's about helping everyone move forward. And setting a culture where little things can be changed without abandoning the big idea. Theologians don't make good product managers. The chief technology officer of a company I worked with was a theologian. He would say, "This is the way it's done." And he was compromised if we didn't do it exactly that way. I worked with some guys in another company who were that way about agile development practices. They would say, "That's not how it's done in agile. And we run agile." I would say, "Gosh, guys, couldn't we just do it that way today, just to get it out the door?"

If you are a theologian, you won't be successful as a product manager. There are a lot of compromises. Moving it forward and making practical trade-off decisions, and working with a lot of theologians. Many people rise to a high level in a technical area and are passionate about the practice and the craft of what they do. Product managers have to work with them. Creative directors are famous for this. As the product manager, you are the one who has to bridge the gap.

WHAT HAPPENS WHEN YOU TRY TO MOVE THE BALL FORWARD AND YOU MAKE A MISTAKE?

When you make a product mistake, you spend equity. If the whole key to your success is, *I'm willing to follow the path laid out by that guy*, and the path doesn't go anywhere, and you backtrack and say, "That wasn't the right path," you only have so many chances. Some people are better than others at acknowledging that, patching it up, and getting people to cut them a break. You have to backtrack and say, "Here's why I thought that was the right path, even though some of you didn't think it was the right path, but you followed me anyway.

Here's what I learned by going down this bad path. I'm not going to say it won't happen again, but I won't make *that* mistake again."

Good product managers are not overly dramatic about their successes or failures. They say, "OK, we did that, it worked, it didn't work." There's a fine line of acknowledging that things didn't work and not dwelling on and defending the choices you made, so you don't look as bad as you really look. Just accept it and move on: "It didn't work. That cost us ninety days. I'll try not to do that again." It's a relief pitcher's mentality. You got roughed up yesterday; you come back in today and forget about it.

WHEN YOU MAKE PRODUCT DECISIONS, IT SEEMS THAT YOU ARE CONSTANTLY AWARE OF DATA COMING FROM PEOPLE AT WORK AND IN THE MARKET, AND FROM USERS. HOW DO YOU BALANCE THE QUANTITATIVE DATA AND QUALITATIVE DATA COMING IN?

I'm a great fan of patterns. One of our product managers hacked together a tiny little visualization of the top schools and profiles on MyEdu, based on the same data that our business intelligence team uses. The insight I got out of thirty seconds from that page was infinitely greater than the mounds of data I'd been pouring through from that same data source. I like when the data has a pattern, and I like to either spend enough time with the data myself to see the pattern or be around people who are good at that.

It's like a bell curve of time. Something that looks simple can be really hard to get people to understand, buy into, and support if they haven't gone over the mountain. But on the other side, it's simple again. It's simplicity on the other side of complexity.

At Procter & Gamble, even in 1997, I had pricing data on my desktop from every retail outlet in the country, statistically significant samples that I could run regressions on until the cows came home. I was there all night doing t-statistics, trying to figure out why Cheer's main SKU unit was losing market share to lower-priced brands in a way that Tide's wasn't. I was awash in the data. That's the first time I ever heard the phrase *analysis paralysis*. My boss at the time said that and suggested that I go talk to the qualitative researchers, who had done a grocery store pricing study. When I talked to them, one nugget came out that opened up the whole pattern for me.

The researchers had done a study—keep in mind, this was 1997—that showed that grocery store customers balked at a $10 price point. They had a mental block that said, "I don't want to spend $10 on anything at the grocery store," which I think still exists, seventeen years later. Our main SKU had just been moved to $9.99, and so had Tide's. But Tide was more heavily discounted and couponed by the retailers themselves, so their list price was $9.99 less often, even though the net for us was the same. The retailers were going from $9.99 to $8.99 on Tide, but they weren't doing it on Cheer. I could see the price fluctuations in the data I had, but I didn't see the consumer behavior related to the price-point issue. I had a whole bunch of data that wasn't showing me anything, and all of the sudden, I saw it with new eyes.

We addressed it simply. We did high-value couponing. We countered one emotional effect of a $9.99 price point with another. P&G had never done a dollar coupon. We had the countereffect: "Wow! A dollar off"—which was a lot for a coupon. And it worked. We patched the sales gap for that quarter, and it was effective in generating more revenue. We countered the optics of that price with the optics of another price.

The point is that the problem was hard to see in the complexity of analytical data. I had to go tease that out, and I didn't know what to look for until I got that insight from the research team.

SO PART OF THE JOB IS LIKE BEING A DETECTIVE?

Yes. I had a friend who used to say it was like being a CIA agent. You get all of this data, and you have to piece it together. What's the puzzle? What does it look like? I'll either create the time for myself to do that or try to be around people who are doing this. They aren't bringing me simple solutions that are on the early side of complexity; they bring me simple solutions that are the results of late nights of analysis.

Still, some people bring you this data in the middle of analysis, saying, "Look at all of the complexity I've identified." But that's not useful. Instead, it's all about what you produce at the other end. It's finding those people and working with them. I don't have to have all the insights. They'll produce really simple statements, but there's a huge analysis that tells you everything about it. Being around people who are good at getting to simple insights advances my ability to make good product decisions. If you have simple insights, you can make better product decisions.

WHAT DO YOU SEE AS THE DIFFERENCE IN PRODUCT DECISIONS MADE BY DESIGNERS COMPARED TO THOSE BY ENGINEERS OR MARKETERS?

What is interesting to me as a product manager is the whole idea of empathetic design. People will tell you that "I'm designing for customers, I'm spending my time with customers, I really understand customers." I had a wacky professor in business school who would say things like, "We don't use the term *love* enough in business. Do you *love* the people you are working with? Do you *love* the customers you are providing solutions for?" The people who are great at these things, the greatest business leaders, are capable of that feeling.

Empathetic design is a more vulnerable approach to thinking about how you build products. It's saying, "I'm willing to more deeply engage with these customers and really empathize with them." It's a mentality of walking in their shoes.

At P&G, there was a creative presentation. They asked me, "What do you think of the copy in the print ad?" I said, "Oh, I like it." Then someone said, "None of us care what you think. Frank, how many loads of laundry do you do in a week?" I said, "One?" "Well, a mother of four does ten. We don't care what you think. We care about what a mother of four thinks about it, and if you don't know, go find some and ask them." Take Swiffer. That was created when I was there out of a notion that we needed new products and we needed to innovate. So the innovation group did in-home visits. They watched people taking a Bounty paper towel after it came out of the dryer and sticking it on the bottom of a broomstick and a mop and dragging it across the floor because it had static and would pick up dust. The participants were talking about how important it was to get every piece of dust on their hardwood floors. The innovation group came back and said, "These people are so passionate about getting the dust off their hardwood floors. How can we help?"

My takeaway is that true empathetic design is where the big ideas are. And product managers want to be associated with big ideas. The good ones don't want to be on the margins. Embracing the humanity is what leads to great products. Not good products, but great, breakthrough, change-the-game products. I think that's been somewhat borne out by the design community. It's not easy to do. It's not fast. It's not cheap. It's not something everybody is comfortable with.

shipping

Joe is in the weeds. His team has committed to a launch date, and he's trying to get as much done as he can in as short a time as possible. He's tempted to cut corners and keeps reminding himself—and his colleagues—about the importance of nailing the details and producing something they can be really proud of.

He senses that some on the team are frustrated. It's been a series of long nights, and while Joe has a mental image of the completed system, there's a wide gap between his aspirations and reality. He closes his eyes and thinks about how he can do a better job of helping everyone see the finish line, even though it's so far away.

BUILDING AND LEVERAGING A PRODUCT ROAD MAP

You've figured out what you are going to build, and you've created artifacts—like the product concept map, hero flows, and mood boards—to help people understand and believe in the product story. There's a second story that needs to be believable, too: how you intend to get the product built and out the door. As the product manager, you'll champion a product road map, which is a visual tool that offers a forward-looking view of capability and strategy changes. You'll use it to manage and communicate the complexity of product decisions, and also to provide visibility into how current tactics map to larger, broader goals. You'll also use the road map as a visual way to build consensus and have conversations about the product over the road map; it becomes a way for others to believe in a vision of the future.

A product road map is a horizontal timeline. The length of time you include depends on the audience for the road map, but a three- or six-month time horizon is realistic. If you try to predict ahead beyond six months, your narrative starts to sound less believable. Particularly in a start-up, six months can include an unexpected liquidity event or a complete redirection of the company. Although it looks similar to a Gantt chart, the product road map isn't a project management tool, so it isn't useful for plotting things at a daily or hourly level of granularity. You won't be able to track things at that level of detail. Instead, the map gives a broad stroke of how a product will come to life over time.

The main components on the road map are capability blocks. Each block represents a building effort, acting as an abstraction of development activities. A block is typically shown as a rectangle, where the width of the rectangle describes how long the development effort will take.

Often, product road maps have swim lanes: horizontal sections that describe, organizationally, who is in charge of a certain development activity.

If you only have a few people writing code, each swim lane may be a single person. If you have a few groups of developers organized in agile scrum teams, each lane may be a team. And if you have a large organization, each lane may be an entire business unit.

The final piece of a road map is the most important, but is the most difficult to visualize. As capability is developed in blocks, the blocks build to enable larger business and user goals. The product road map should show how a piece of functionality is tied to these goals and should visually connect the dots to show the strategic importance of building certain things in a sequence.

START BY BUILDING A CAPABILITY LIST

Build the product road map in phases. First, think about your product in its most complete state—with all the bells and whistles—and list all of the capabilities enabled by the product. Use your noun-verb pairs from the hero flows as a starting point, but broaden them to include both what a person will do with the system and what the system will do by itself. This is your capability list.

Recall Joe's insight statement: *People are generally aware of the stress in their jobs, but aren't specifically aware of the stress at any given moment or day. They feel the cumulative emotional burden of stress only after it's too late to do anything about it. **There should be a way for people to see day-to-day changes in their stress, so they can constantly adjust their behavior in an ongoing fashion**.*

Based on the insight statement, he's made a series of product design artifacts, so he can create a capability list that looks like this:

- Send text messages.
- Receive text messages.
- Pull in athlete data from Nike+.

- Pull in athlete data from Fitbit.
- Pull in social data from Facebook.
- Pull in social data from Twitter.
- Create visualization of insights.

In addition to these capabilities that directly drive user value, there are also a series of maintenance capabilities that are important to include:

- Sign-up
- Log-in and authentication
- Transaction and e-commerce (credit card processing)

These capabilities are considered maintenance because they don't necessarily require innovation or even creative thinking. You need to account for them on the road map because they will take development resources and time.

First, ignore time.

Create a first draft of your road map. On a large sheet of paper, oriented horizontally, draw a timeline, but don't label the time units. Think of it as a generic segment of time. Use Post-it notes to represent each capability so that you can move them around on the road map. Create a Post-it note for the end state when all of your capabilities are implemented. Label it "version 1.0" and below that write "Entire capability list implemented." Place the Post-it note all the way on the right side of the road map.

Draw horizontal rows to indicate the swim lanes of engineering resources you can leverage. If your company has three developers who work on your team, make three rows. Unless you are directly responsible for managing the developers, don't put names on the rows: resource allocation is probably not your decision to make. You'll work with the engineering lead to identify who is doing what later. For now, just identify the number of people that you have who can work in parallel.

Now, write each capability from the list on a unique Post-it note, and place each note on the road map in a sequence and grouping that makes sense. For example, it seems logical that the developer who creates the ability of the system to send messages should also create the ability of the system to receive messages, so those capabilities can be grouped together on the same row. Those capabilities are distinct efforts, so they need to be prioritized; one has to happen before the other.

The art and science of managing a road map is identifying the capability as a discrete and chunkable item, grouping it with other similar items, and prioritizing the sequence of items relative to one another. As you examine each capability, compare it to your value proposition and ask yourself, "Can you achieve the value proposition without this capability?" If the answer is yes, shift the capability to the right. If the answer is no, shift it to the left. The items on the left become prioritized higher so they get completed first. Joe's draft road map is shown in figure 6-1.

Add time to the road map.

Now comes the hard part: getting other people to understand your road map and working with those people to add realism. Show your road map in its "no-time" state to the various developers and engineers in informal, one-on-one meetings. Engage the actual people who will write the code, not just the manager or team lead. Present the road map as a draft, and ask for their help and feedback. As you walk through each capability, they'll ask questions and ask for clarifications. Use the other artifacts you've developed to answer those questions. Walk through the hero flow wireframes with them. Present the product concept map. Tell them the

Figure 6-1

Joe's draft of a road map

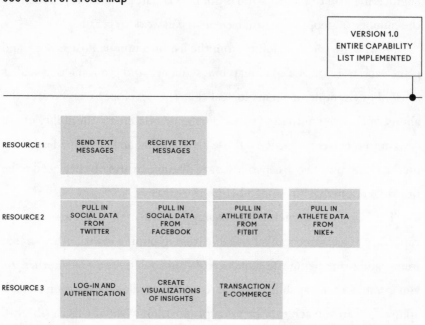

story of how the product you are going to build will provide that deep emotional value to people and find out what they think of that story.

Ask if your prioritization and order make sense and explain the sequencing you've selected. If they suggest changes to the sequencing, take their suggestions to heart and consider reordering things. The people who will actually be doing the work need to understand and respect the road map decisions you've made, and the best way for them to respect it is to contribute to it. Consider making the changes to the road map in front of them, so they actually see you that you value their input and opinion.

Now, ask them to add time to the road map, using their best guesses. You can't believe their guesses; they'll be way off. Your goal, at this stage, is to get a baseline estimate—a broad understanding of what your team *thinks* might be done by certain milestones (typically, monthly or in three-month increments). Watch team members work and compare their pace with their estimates; then, over time, you can develop a sense for how long your team will *actually* take to produce new functionality. For now, your intent is to have a plan that everyone agrees is a good idea—a plan that they respect, understand, and want to work hard to achieve. After working with engineering, Joe's final road map looks the one shown in figure 6-2.

The road map is a living document: it's never really finished. It will adapt to the changing needs of the business and to the evolving product vision, and it will have to adapt based on delays or unexpected events in development productivity. Changes to the road map need to be managed to make sure everyone both understands the changes and believes in them. "Owning the road map" doesn't mean making all of the decisions. You'll

Figure 6-2

Joe's final road map

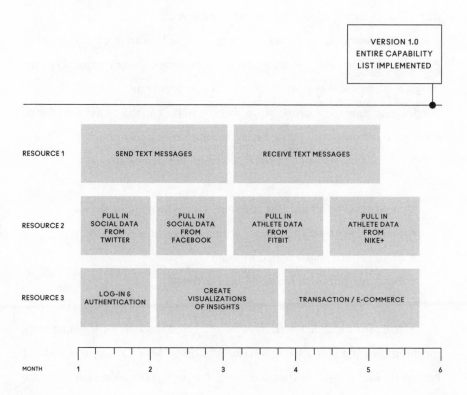

be most successful when you can capture everyone else's decisions and present them cleanly. You'll use the road map constantly in order to make both strategic and tactical decisions.

MOVING FROM THE IDEAL TO THE ACHIEVABLE THROUGH ITERATIONS

Until now you've been painting a picture of the ideal. You've used insights to define a product that has emotional appeal, and you've defined a broad set of capabilities and interactions to help people experience that appeal. When you first start to use your road map and see the pace of your team, you'll realize that achieving the vision may take much longer than you expected. In my earlier example, it would take nearly six months to achieve all of the functionality described as "version 1.0." You need to start to move from the ideal to the achievable. The common way of doing this is to eliminate broad sets of functionality or to cut corners, and you don't really want to do either of these. Instead, assume each capability goes through several development phases. Separate a single capability into iterative phases and spread those phases out over time.

Joe can start to be much more specific in his capability list in order to separate out pieces and make each capability block shorter.

Send text messages can be broken into smaller capabilities:

- Send texts to all users at the same time throughout the day.
- Send texts at various times, when the user schedules them.
- Send generic, hard-coded message.
- Send custom texts based on user activity.

These four capabilities can now be scattered throughout the road map, meaning that Joe can achieve a basic version of *Send text messages* without having to wait for all of that functionality to be built. You can leverage iterations in order to make quick functional strides without abandoning the breadth of the road map. You can paint a broad stroke across *all* functionality and then go back to refine the details of individual features later.

TRANSLATING CAPABILITIES TO STORIES

Each Post-it note on the road map is a placeholder for production activities, like planning, creating graphic assets, writing copy, coding, testing, and a host of other activities. A number of software packages can help you organize all these production activities. What's most important is not the tool you use, but that you provide meaningful structure to illustrate how all these activities come together to achieve the product vision. You can create this structure by writing user stories. Just as the hero flow painted a compelling picture of how someone would use the product to achieve his goals, user stories describe how a particular capability will work from the perspective of the person who uses your product. User stories zoom in to the hero flow in order to describe each step of the flow in more detail. This is where broad design decisions become specific feature requirements.

Recall that one of Joe's main hero flows went like this:

The screen displays her monthly emotions in a graph, showing two periods that fall below the average. She taps a button labeled, "Analyze My Life," and the app explains that her emotions seem to fall every Tuesday around 3 p.m. It also shows that, based on her iOS calendar, she has a meeting every Tuesday from 2 to 3 p.m. with a specific coworker. The one week that the meeting was canceled, her emotions didn't fall. "Interesting . . ." Mary thinks to herself.

And, remember that Joe has a single capability called

Create visualization of insights.

Joe can piece together the hero flow and the capability in order to write these user stories:

- **The user should be able to view a graph that displays her emotions over time**. The graph should display time on the x-axis and her emotional responses (gathered via text message) on the y-axis.
- **The user should be able to ask the system to analyze the graph**. The system should apply a series of algorithmic analysis tools to the data in order to identify trends or anomalies.
- **The user should be able to easily identify periods that are particularly high or low on the emotion graph**. The graph should use color to highlight highs or lows, so they are visible at a glance.
- **The user should be able to visually compare the emotion graph to regular activities on the calendar app on her phone**. The system should identify places where calendar events coincide with highs, lows, or anomalies on the graph. The user should be able to tap on those places and view a link between the calendar event and the emotional moment.

Note that the stories act as a bridge between capability and feature. Now, a designer can create wireframes or visual renderings to support this specific feature. A copywriter can produce the text that a user will see. Marketing can produce advertising collateral to highlight these features, and development can start to strategize how to code to support these features. The stories don't answer all the questions, and in many ways, the stories provoke *more* questions to be answered. But at each stage, from hero flow to capability to user story, you are working to answer the question, *What should we build?* These tools answer that question by putting boundaries around a blank canvas, and they force an answer that is always focused on the user.

PRIORITIZING FUNCTIONALITY AND MANAGING A BACKLOG OF GOOD IDEAS

Once you have a functioning product, you'll inevitably have countless ideas for how to improve and expand it. Because design is generative, you'll always have more good ideas than you can possibly deliver on; your largest constraint quickly becomes the amount of engineering capacity available for you to leverage. You need to manage a list of all the good ideas and find a way to have them defined, designed, and ready to build when engineering resources become available.

That list is called your product backlog. It's a living, breathing list that is constantly changing as you acquire new information about how people are using your product. You manage it by prioritizing ideas and removing things that are no longer relevant. That pruning should happen regularly. I've found it useful to review the backlog every day and set aside time specifically to prune it once a week.

Your product backlog has another purpose, too. It becomes a way for you to depoliticize functionality suggestions. Everyone in the company will have new ideas for your product, and while well intentioned, many of the ideas just aren't any good. They may not fit with the emotional value proposition of the product, or they may contradict a larger behavioral goal you've identified. You might be tempted to challenge these ideas and debate why they should or shouldn't be included. A better way to handle left-field suggestions is to include them in the product backlog, but prioritize them toward the bottom. When someone offers you what he thinks is a great new idea, suspend judgment and let him know you've added it to the backlog of potential product features. He'll feel as though he has contributed, and you'll be able to show him that you are considering his idea.

At a broad level, one of the most effective ways to prioritize your backlog is to rank the ideas based on how much they support your emotional value proposition. The backlog should include specific marketing activities, new features or functions, or legacy code that may need to be rewritten. These changes may not directly align with the emotional value you are trying to drive, and that's fine. It's more important that you have a guiding North Star that you can use as a thematic filter for ideas. When all of your development activities stop aligning with that North Star, you need to realign engineering efforts toward your goal.

PUBLICLY TRACKING USER VALUE

Once real people are using your product, you can start to understand if you are achieving what you set out to achieve—if you are delivering on the emotional value proposition. Recall that the emotional value proposition was identified as *something that a person felt after using or acquiring your product, that they couldn't feel before using or acquiring your product*. That emotive value becomes your goal, but it's hard to know for sure if you are achieving that goal. You can establish some metrics that help you make an educated guess, and they can act as guiding indicators of value.

Consider that Joe's emotional value proposition was stated as:

After using LiveWell, people will feel more connected with their body rhythms and will feel more in control of their mental health.

CARING ABOUT TINY, TINY THINGS

Development of interface details can be tedious, particularly at the end of the process when issues of cross-browser compatibility or tiny interface eccentricities start to arise. At this point, you'll find a natural tendency to call it "good enough." The team is fatigued and ready to see its work launch.

A design-driven approach to product development means caring about all the details that a human encounters when he or she uses your product, because these small details have large impacts on the experiences people have. The details include aesthetics, usability issues, language and content, pricing, and issues of information hierarchy. The list is exhausting, and at this point, it's easy to let the details fall apart. Sometimes they seem to fall apart slowly, as people's attention turns to new capabilities and new ideas. Other times, they fall apart all at once, because the details aren't managed through the product launch. If you want other people to care about details, you have to care about them yourself. There's no shortcut or trick to this, and because there are so many details, you need to be constantly in the weeds.

Keep lists.

When a designer shows you a screen mock-up with dummy text, or a developer demos some code for you that isn't visually resolved, add the details to a running, written list. Then, be sure to circle back in a few days to ask how the text or code was completed. Polish the details through your product and pleasantly surprise people when you remember and follow up with them.

Track visual and usability defects.

In a typical bug-tracking system, visual defects are given the lowest priority ("Oh, that's just cosmetic, so we can fix that last"), and usability defects don't even rank. However, for hitting your metrics, a visual issue can be as critical as a broken piece of code. You can increase your development team's awareness (and respect) of design details by opening defects against both usability and visual issues in your product and ranking them in the same manner as functional defects. Include the reason for your prioritizing in the description of the defect because it won't be obvious to developers. Why code that doesn't function properly should be fixed is obvious. It's not always evident why poorly aligned images are worth fixing, particularly with limited development resources. You need to explain how consistency, visual acuity, and polish have an impact on trust, and how trust is critical to the product's success.

Produce relevant design documentation.

Only one thing is worse than writing a design spec and that's reading one. Trying to document every single design decision drives both you and your development team crazy and wastes time because it's much easier to work through detailed design on the screen, sitting next to a developer and talking through interactions. Some specific design details are important to document; a series of five lightweight and midweight artifacts can do the job without resorting to a full spec:

1. Produce a bubble diagram that displays the hero path, show-ing how one screen leads to the next. This helps the developers create routes and helps them understand how data must move through the system. (See figure 6-3.)

Figure 6-3

Bubble diagram of the hero path

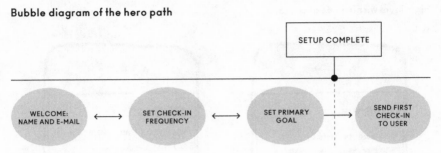

2. Produce a series of high-level wireframes that describe the screens users encounter. These help the developers understand what back-end services are used and begin to describe the complexity of the presentation layer. (See figure 6-4.)

3. Create detailed wireframes for specific critical interactions, such as a control that is used on every page (navigation), one that's fundamental to success (a shopping cart), or one that's extremely intricate. (See figure 6-5.)

4. Create a visual design document (a pixel-perfect comp) that shows the most important screens. Typically, five or ten screens are enough to help the development team see the variety of screen types you intend and to provide sufficient data to scope out a front-end development effort. Redline these documents to add specifications for padding, margin, font sizes, and other visual elements and to put these specifications directly on top of the comp (in red, hence the name). (See figure 6-6.)

5. Create a visual design tear sheet of every standard platform component and control (that is, textboxes, checkboxes, radio buttons) and all nonstandard components and controls that you intend to use throughout the product. Redline the tear sheet, just

Figure 6-4

High-level wireframes of screens

Figure 6-5

Visual comps of key screens

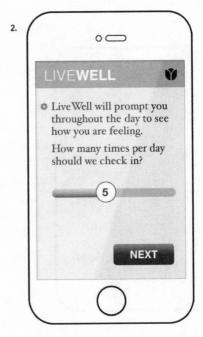

Figure 6-6

Redline specifications

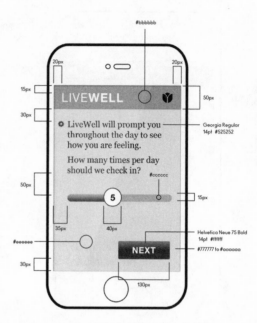

as you did with the comps. Then have the development team code the entire sheet, so it has a standard set of controls it can reference throughout. (See figure 6-7.)

TEACHING AND EVANGELIZING

Learning to see and care about details is one thing. Getting everyone else on the team to care about them is another. Part of your job is that of an educator—teaching the other members of your team to see the world in a new way, one in which small nuances add up to a larger whole.

Figure 6-7

Visual design tear sheet with components and controls

Help developers to see.

Developers generally have been trained to see the world through a lens of functionality. They'll notice the way things work, but they typically won't see the way things look. If you are trying to achieve a certain level of visual polish, fit, and finish, that can be particularly frustrating. Your developers literally may be unable to notice any difference between an 80 percent approximation of your comp and the comp itself. Even when you prepare a redlined version of a given design, complete with pixel counts and font-size specifications, some developers still won't realize that what they've coded only approximates the specification.

You can help developers learn to see the differences between an approximation of a design and a pixel-perfect design with a simple trick. Take a screen shot of their work and overlay your comp on top of it at 50 percent opacity to show any differences between their work and your vision. Explain the difference to the developers and why each detail matters. It's not enough that someone sees what you see. He needs to understand why your view of the world is important and why these visual details matter. If you can help him see that you made visual design decisions purposefully and methodically, and that they support a larger goal, he'll help you realize your aesthetic vision.

Set an example.

Holding everyone up to a high standard and failing to meet that standard yourself is not fair. If you are going to constantly remind people to be more detail oriented, you need to push yourself to be more detail oriented, too. Zoom in on your own work—your backlog, requirement definition, user stories, wireframes, or any other artifact you make—to sweat the details.

TAKING A PROACTIVE STANCE

With few exceptions, market activities don't just happen. Someone *makes* them happen by taking an action, making a comment, or reacting to an event. Product management requires a proactive stance on the way you want the market to receive your product. You don't control other people and you certainly don't control the market, but you can try to increase your chances of success.

Ask yourself what action you can take to get a desired outcome. Are you hoping for an article about your product in an influential tech journal?

You could wait for a reporter to discover your product on her own, or you could let her know the product exists. Are you hoping users discover and use a new functionality you've launched? Rather than waiting for them to stumble upon it, consider how you can present cues within the product to guide them there. Are you concerned that your team isn't operating as fast as it needs to? Think about what action you can take to incent them to move faster. Product management is a role of volition. While you may find yourself responding to inputs and activities, your role is one that's strikingly proactive.

SHORT-CIRCUITING DEBATE WITH ARTIFACTS

People's opinions about what to do and how to do it will conflict at each step of the development process. Collaborative creativity is often a highly emotional process. People feel exposed when they make a public statement about a new idea. They've made a prediction and tied their own worth to that vision of the future. If their idea isn't supported, they may feel as though they've been personally or professionally slighted. They have ownership of that idea, and that ownership is a powerful emotional force.

People may argue in support of an idea even when presented with a rational argument *against* it, so verbal debate can become circular or endless. Such debate can be a tremendous waste of time because capturing the nuance or specificity of a product decision in language is difficult. Words may not have enough richness to capture product decisions. You may find yourself arguing with someone for the same idea, in what is often called violent agreement.

You can short-circuit endless debates over features, functions, and design details by making *things*. The thing can be a diagram, a sketch, or a high-level fidelity design artifact. When you make a thing, an idea becomes real.

A thing says, "I mean this, and not that"; it's a way of formalizing intent and reducing ambiguity.

Making things *during* a discussion or debate is a wonderful way to establish consensus and minimize circular arguments. After the conversation is over, the thing remains as a log or reminder of what everyone agreed upon. A week or a month after the meeting, you'll be able to quickly relive the entire debate by looking at the artifact; it will act as a proxy for the conversation. Working on a whiteboard is a simple way to move a conversation from spoken word to artifact. You can train yourself and your teams to grab a whiteboard marker and to force conversations into a visual medium.

BRINGING IDEAS TO LIFE BY SOCIALIZATION

Part of your role is making sure everyone in your organization knows what product decisions are being made, and why they are being made the way they are. Preston Smalley, executive director of product management at Comcast, spent much of his career at eBay. He commented:

> The goal is always partnership. You want to be in a situation where marketing understands your important role, and you understand their important role. Where I've seen it go wrong is when marketing feels like product is there to do their bidding, or the other way around—where product feels like they just need to kick something to marketing a few weeks before launch, without awareness of how they do their job. Neither of those models works very well. If you can create an environment where people feel listened to, they'll reciprocate. I saw this at eBay. I would reach across to talk to marketing, and you thought an alien had landed in their area. They had never had a deep conversation with someone in product or design, and they were thrilled to be doing that.[1]

Even in a small company, it can become difficult to keep track of all the different things that are happening, and a lack of product alignment can lead to logistical problems or emotional resentment. You can help ensure product alignment by actively socializing your product road map—by shopping it around the company, describing what's coming, and soliciting feedback and input on future direction and changes. When you share your product road map, you need to understand each individual's motivations and incentives and speak directly to these. Show how the product decisions you've made support their goals and objectives. For example, if your sales team is rewarded on a commission basis, you need to know how the product changes you are driving will help the team close additional sales. You'll only know this if you've spent time with it early in the process.

Fundamentally, your act of socialization should paint a clear story of how your planned product changes support a larger business story or intent. You should be able to easily connect the product decisions you are making to the strategic goals of the company, and the best way to do that is to connect them directly to your emotional value proposition. Explain how any new feature, flow, or product change helps your users better feel the things you want them to feel.

ESTABLISHING A LAUNCH CADENCE

When you start caring about details, you'll find that things take longer—a lot longer. You might be tempted to focus exclusively on a set of features or new product functionality, polishing it until it's perfect. But a regular launch cadence for interim releases—reviewing and pushing code live once a week, or even several times a day—gives you the ability to make changes quickly. If you find something wrong with your product, you can prioritize changes and push them out as soon as they are complete, rather than waiting to align your changes to a larger monthly or quarterly development release cycle.

Most importantly, regular launches drive a sense that the product is malleable, and that it can change based on people's input, ideas, or innovations. Your team needs to feel that it is making forward progress, and launching products regularly helps drive positive internal momentum. Philosophically, daily releases help your team claim emotional ownership of the product and feel empowered to make changes to it.

MOTIVATING ENGINEERS

In addition to supporting a fluid and constant release cycle, you can help your engineering team remain motivated by making it clear why you are asking the team to build the various product changes you have planned. A simple way to do this is to include a *rationale* for each item on the road map and clearly describe how it provides additional emotional or utilitarian value to your users.

Additionally, you can help motivate engineers by providing measurable indicators of success for each item on the road map. Before you begin development efforts, help your engineering team understand what determines the success of a given effort. What behavior will you track? How will you track that behavior? And what goals do you have for that metric to indicate if it's working as desired? You may find these values to be intuitive or obvious, and think they are not worth measuring. But your developers are highly analytical, and providing them with a clear quantitative measurement to track helps them understand the relevance of their work and judge its success.

SNIFFING OUT USER BEHAVIOR FROM USAGE DATA

Once people are using your product, you'll be astounded at how exciting (and, often, confusing) it can be to look at usage data and try to understand what they were doing and why they were doing it. You'll have hundreds or thousands of analytics data points; in the richest scenario, you'll be able to recreate what each user did with your product, although you won't have the time to do it because it would take you thousands of hours.

Leverage usage data to inform product changes, but optimize the time you spend with analytics. To do this, tie your analytics queries directly to your emotional value proposition and corresponding success metrics. Recall that Joe had defined the happy customer percentage and global wellness number as the two metrics he would track. He should spend time thoroughly establishing ways to track these metrics in whatever analytics package his company is using and then do his best to resist the pressure to measure anything and everything else. Measurement is a zero-sum game, and lost time is the cost of additional and extraneous analytics.

Try to dedicate a set portion of your time for free-form analytics analysis—for "playing with your data." An hour a week helps you identify unexpected patterns or trends, and gives you time for serendipitously stumbling upon new behavioral data.

When your numbers start changing or if they aren't where you want them to be, you'll naturally want to understand why. While the cause may be obvious—you may have launched a new piece of functionality—the cause can also be hidden or difficult to isolate. Causality can be hidden in the tiniest of interface details, and changes to extremely simple design elements can drive large changes in a product. According to interface folklore about the $300 million button design, a simple interface change led to a massive increase in revenue for an online retailer.[2] Not all of your design decisions will have nearly that level of direct impact. But tiny changes—like smartly selecting default choices, or auto-focusing the mouse cursor on the first interface element—have an impact, and when you have a lot of traffic to your product, you'll start to see how a small change can amplify into large results.

READING EVERY SUPPORT TICKET

Dedicate some of your road map to launching a hosted help solution—a tool that allows your customers to ask for help in a structured format. Then read every single request for support that comes in. You'll start to understand behavioral trends and find that you can intuitively understand how product changes are having an impact on product usage. You can use feedback from the customer support process to drive new product changes. Be careful though and resist the urge to automatically change the product based on every single comment you get. You'll have to judge each request to really understand if it represents a larger product problem.

CELEBRATING VICTORIES

A product manager is said to be someone who brings the doughnuts on the day of the release. Celebrate the victories of your team, because it's so easy to lose track of progress or lose sight of your goals. As you've seen, building a product is hard work and takes time, dedication, and passion. The process is emotionally all-encompassing. You and your team need to care deeply about the product in order to deliver the emotional value you've promised your users. If you care that deeply, you'll inevitably feel as though the product is part of you—an extension of your being. Launching new products or achieving significant usage milestones are cause for celebration and reflection, and for pride. Product design is hard, hard work. You deserve to feel good about your accomplishments, and so does your entire team.

AN INTERVIEW WITH ALEX RAINERT, ON GROWING A PRODUCT AND A BUSINESS

Alex Rainert is head of product at Foursquare. He brings fifteen years of product development experience and a multidisciplinary background to his work, with a focus on mobile, social, and emerging technologies. Previously, he cofounded Dodgeball, one of the first mobile social services in the United States, and sold it to Google in May 2005. He's obsessed with design, emerging technologies, sports, and food. He blogs about all sorts of things at alexrainert .com. He is a lifelong New Yorker currently living in Brooklyn with his wife, daughter, and dog. Rainert holds a master's degree from New York University's interactive telecommunications program and a bachelor's degree in philosophy from Trinity College.

ALEX, TELL ME ABOUT SOME OF YOUR HISTORY AT FOURSQUARE.

I'm the head of product at Foursquare. Product contains product management, the design team, and the platform team. All three groups are close to anyone external who interfaces with the brand directly. Whether it's through the apps, the site, or the API—it's the thread that holds them all together.

WHAT'S THE SHORT ANSWER TO WHAT DO YOU DO? WHAT IS PRODUCT MANAGEMENT?

I set the stage for people to do their best work. That's like giving directions, giving feedback, unblocking them, getting them talking to the right people, facilitating creativity across teams.

IS THAT SOMETHING THAT CAN BE TAUGHT?

You learn this when you work on team projects. Certainly, you learn it at agencies. I feel this every time I interview designers from agencies to work at a start-up. People have to go through a big shift. At an agency, engineering is seen as the boundaries, but at start-ups, it's the enabler. I would say, "Oh, we want to do this thing, but tech can't do it." People come here and we can literally build anything. The burden is on thinking creatively. Don't worry about how to build it; we can build it. It's a different mind-set. People who have been on the agency side for a long time have an unseen boundary on how widely they think about things.

Any time you are working in teams, where people have different roles, you learn the dynamics and challenges of consensus building, which is a big part of product management. Some product managers struggle with this. It's not about making *your* idea happen. It's about helping the *best* idea happen. You have to, as a product manager, be able to separate yourself from the problem. Some people might never be able to do it. Others learn to compartmentalize over time and say, "Hey, I would do it this way, but I understand that everyone else is making a case to go that other way, so I'll let it go."

Teams really appreciate that. When they can see a product manager do that, and they can see that they are there to help the team do its best work and the work that they are most proud of. Their opinions don't get in the way of that.

YOU'RE DESCRIBING COMPROMISE. IT SOUNDS AS IF A BIG PART OF PRODUCT MANAGEMENT, FOR YOU, IS COMPROMISING VISION. THAT'S THE OPPOSITE OF

WHAT WE HEAR ABOUT FROM CEOS AND OTHER PRODUCT LUMINARIES, LIKE STEVE JOBS. DO YOU THINK JOBS WAS A PRODUCT MANAGER?

No. He would have had his way in what he wanted, and that was it. It's about how an organization runs. If you have that type of company, the people you are working with have to be comfortable with that kind of organization. I've seen design teams with one creative director and fifteen production people. That works for a lot of people, and as long as everyone there is onboard with it, that's great. But you run into problems when you try to shift in midstream. People may say, "Hey, I thought we were hired to try to solve problems and now you are just telling me what to build." That's where companies run into problems.

THAT PROBABLY HAPPENS NATURALLY DURING THAT GROWTH PERIOD. YOU HAVE TO SHIFT TO A PRODUCTION MIND-SET.

Right, and a shared understanding of what you are doing. It's how you build in a system of empowerment and accountability as the organization grows. We have all these teams, and every week we have a meeting with the design leads. They say, "Here's what we're working on. Is this in line with what you think is important?" We might do level setting around it. They own their road map, but there are checks and balances along the way, so that everyone agrees that we are working on the most important things.

When I joined the company, there were twelve people. Before I got here, the product team was one designer and Dennis, the CEO. Initially I came on part-time to help out with anything—product management, or wireframes, whatever needed to happen. When you are all sitting around the table, everyone gets it. With Dodgeball [a previous social networking product], our most explicit road map was a text file, or some combination of a text file and a whiteboard. Now, there are more levels in the organization, and the product is much more complex.

The different teams working on different parts need to be in sync. Those are problems you just don't have when the company has only twelve people.

I came on more formally to build out the product team. I had a visual designer, and I hired a product manager and a user-experience designer. I had one core atomic unit of a team that could tackle anything. From there, I continued to try to replicate that model: user experience, visual designer, and product manager working together. As the company got larger, I was able to give each of those pods more focus. One focused on merchant tools; one focused on the consumer app. The roles changed over time, because roughly every time you double in size, the way you get anything done has to change. The way you collaborate, the way you make decisions, especially at the speed at which start-ups grow, is a very fragile process. You have to be flexible with it and be OK with the fact that it will break, as long as you learn how to make it better.

Now we have 140 people and a lot of my job is making sure that the machine is designed properly to ensure that the product is designed properly. We have eighty-five engineers and about fifteen people on the product team. Thirty percent of the engineers came to us from Google, so it's a very engineering-heavy culture. From day one, we wanted product and engineering to go hand in hand. In some organizations, product reports to engineering. In others, like Zynga, the product manager is the CEO; he decides what will happen and engineering executes. It's been important to us to have that balance. Our vice president of engineering, Harry Heymann, and I have always been peers. We've tried to figure out how to get the teams to work together. As the company has gotten bigger, our challenge has been: how do you make a road map when you have 150 people? How do you find the balance between empowering people and also holding them accountable for what they do? Those are some of the toughest problems, because people want the North Star for what needs to be built, but they also don't want to be told what to build.

A lot of this is the black art of product management. When we had eighty people, we created smaller cross-disciplinary teams. Each team was focused on one problem the company was trying to solve, like getting our users to create more content on the service. Our hope was that if employees had the resources they needed to build and ship, and a clear area of focus, they would be empowered to go after that and to really marinate in a problem set over time.

It was an effort to avoid the launch-and-forget problem. When we launched photos and comments, the team moved on to work on lists and then on to Explorer. Meanwhile, no one had done anything to photos and comments in six months. So our intention in giving these teams a clear area of focus was that they could do the maintenance and ongoing improvement to the stuff they were working on. We learned that a structure like that was awesome for iterative improvement, but we needed to build in space and time to think bigger than in incremental improvements.

We've learned so much in the three-and-a-half years that I've been there, and things have drastically changed in that time. I need to recognize when something doesn't work and then avoid making the same mistake twice. But it's impossible to make no mistakes, especially if you are going to grow at the rate of most start-ups.

A THEME IN START-UPS IS THAT IDEA OF "MAKING MISTAKES IN ORDER TO LEARN," AND THAT YOU HAVE TO HAVE A FEW FAILED START-UPS UNDER YOUR BELT ALMOST AS A FORM OF CREDIBILITY. IS THAT REALLY NECESSARY?

You don't necessarily have to go through failing with an entire product. But you learn more when times are tough than when times are easy. When you are shipping stuff, and the tech press can say nothing but good things about you, it's fun, but it's not hard product work. It's hard product work when you have to figure out how to turn a start-up into a business, and when certain things aren't working and you have to really dig into them. You look at data and do research; you need to really dig into why users are or are not doing something. That's something that's hard, early on in start-ups, and you grow into that. We struggled with some of our infrastructure, and over the years, we've gotten into a much better place in terms of analytics. And we hired a user-experience researcher; that's been a great two-pronged attack at a lot of product things. We just didn't have those things when the company was six months old. Those are things that, early on, a lot of companies treat like a luxury. But by the time you realize you need them, you actually needed them six months ago.

Talking to people who have already gone through it makes a huge difference, too. But the industry is so young that it's hard to find people who have had shared experiences. There aren't a lot of examples of people who have gone through the whole process; how do you take a product, turn it into a start-up, turn it into a company, turn it into an organization? It's hard to find people who have experiences to share with those four giant steps. Finding them is incredibly valuable. It's easy to feel that "oh my god, the problems we are going through are so unique."

WHAT ROLE DOES THE PRODUCT ORGANIZATION PLAY IN SOLVING THOSE PROBLEMS?

For better or for worse, product is the discipline that sits at the hub of the wheel. You need people who can work with designers, engineers, marketing, business development. But at the same time, you deal with the challenges of all of those different areas. Even within those groups, people have different needs. You have engineers who are very product minded and just need high-level outlines of the problem you are trying to solve, and they'll run with it. Then you have others who need a spec before they start building. If you give them the edge cases, they'll go crush it. For a product manager to know how to tune his approach based on the problem, the individuals, and the combination of individuals he is working with is a huge part of the role.

I have more of a design approach to organizing my group. After three-and-a-half years of trying to hire other product managers, I've had a hard time finding people who haven't had the Google APM experience. It's important to me to find that strong analytical ability that Google is really good at honing, but it can't be at the expense of the feel and passion of design. Yes, some of the problems we're solving are very algorithm-driven problems, but for the most part, we have a consumer, social product, and we need people who understand that side. They need to understand the high-touch side of the product. A big thing for me is making sure that the design passion and instinct are there in the people I hire. They don't have to have to go design something, but they need to be able to articulate why something solves the problem for the user better than something else, and their rationale can't just be tied to engineering.

My product managers should have the best understanding of the user's problem that we're trying to solve. You get really good at defining why we are building this, without getting into solving the problem. That's a skill that product managers hone over time—being able to articulate what it is we are trying to go after. They are able to look at a design, work with designers, and say, "This is great, but I don't think it solves the problem due to x, y, and z." They articulate that so a designer can take that feedback and turn it into something else. It's not, "That button should be blue and not red"; it's about framing the feedback in a way that asks, "Does this solve the problem we are trying to solve?" Product managers have to be able to frame the problem up front and get everyone on the same page. If there isn't a shared understanding of what the problem is, you can literally debate the solution forever. No one will be wrong. So before we dive into something, we have to get the organization to understand that we all agree. Then we can look at design solutions and frame them within that problem. But if we're just looking at different interfaces with no clear framework, then it just becomes opinions.

YOU'VE DONE AGENCY WORK, TOO. HAS YOUR CONSULTING BACKGROUND HELPED YOUR PRODUCT ABILITIES?

Yes, in a lot of different ways. There are a lot of parallels to how you work at an agency, especially on the creative side, to how you work in a start-up. You are always trying to do more with what you have, it's always moving incredibly fast, and the bonus is that you aren't just throwing things over a wall. You get to keep making things better. Once you have the taste of having no layers between you and the end user, it's like a drug.

I started on the agency side and did a start-up, and then an agency, and now I'm at start-up. There are challenges on both sides that I find appealing. But now, you can ship something and in five minutes have people saying, "This sucks," or "This is awesome." For designers, it's like a drug. In an agency, when you work on a project, you have a creative director, and management at the company, and management at the client; by the time you get to the user, it doesn't matter anymore. You've built something, handed it over, and more often than not, you never find out how it did.

HOW DO YOU FIND OUT HOW YOU DID NOW?

We have a user-experience researcher who's always working on something. It could be a specific feature or foundational research. Her presentations on research findings are by far the best meetings of the week. It took us a long time to hire someone for that role, but the organization was hungry for it. Seeing how much people want to hear what she's learning is awesome.

Feedback from as many places as possible is great. But there's also a need to try to maintain balance. Not every piece of feedback is something you need to do something about. That can be hard. We'll "dogfood" a lot of our work before it goes out, resulting in a giant Google doc of feedback that can be overwhelming. It's hard to find the right balance, particularly internally, because we want feedback from everyone. But that doesn't mean we're going to do something about every piece of feedback. The designer and the product manager have a vision for what the product should be.

When the company had twenty people, we would have meetings and make product decisions together. That's insane now. One of the things that has changed as we grow is that we ship features, and not everyone in the company would have designed the features in that way. Or, they might not even want to have the feature in the product. It's important to have a clear reason for product decisions and to be able to articulate it. People may not agree with it or they wouldn't have done it themselves, but they should at least understand how we ended up here and what the rationale is. These are communication skills that you have to hone as you get bigger.

IN THE HISTORY OF YOUR COMPANY, WAS THERE A POINT IN GROWTH WHEN IT OCCURRED TO YOU THAT YOU WERE A "BIG COMPANY"?

Sometimes it feels that way, when too much time is spent on making sure the right people are talking, instead of them just talking. You can't take for granted that someone on this side of the office knows what's going on over on that side of the office. So we build things in. Every Tuesday, we have a company meeting; I started having one or two of the product teams present the most interesting stuff they've been working on in the last few weeks.

You can do mailing lists for the different teams, but that's a lot of stuff to follow. If there are ways to systematize the communication of what's going on, it's super helpful. We've inherited a few things from Google. We do weekly snippets; every Monday, an e-mail goes out to everyone in the company saying, "What did you do last week, and what are you working on this coming week?" Everyone replies to the e-mail, and a digest goes back to the whole company. You can subscribe to different people or groups for a quick way to get a snapshot of what the teams are working on. It's a good way to get around the fact that not everyone is in the same meetings anymore, because the company is bigger. So you have to weigh that balance. You don't want three different e-mail lists to keep up with, where you are doing stand-ups three times a day. All of the sudden you are spending all of your time communicating. Find the right tools that work for the people you've got to make sure that the right people are talking.

HOW DO YOU BRIDGE THE COMMUNICATION GAP BETWEEN ANALYTICAL ENGINEERS AND EMOTIVE OR EMPATHETIC DESIGNERS?

Companies exist on a spectrum. On the one end is Apple or Path—where everything that gets pushed out is meticulously thought through. It's what you think of as a designer's dream. And on the other end, you have Google with its forty shades of blue. It has come far since then, but you still have this attitude of "ship it and fix it, ship it and fix it." Three or four years ago that was a designer's nightmare. And you have Facebook somewhere in the middle; it tries to toe the line between "move fast and break things," but also "make beautiful things." You need to come to terms with the type of organization you want to be, and one isn't better than the other. But the people need to be onboard with the kind of company you are, because otherwise you are swimming upstream. If you have someone coming from the perfectionist, design-heavy side, and you throw them on the other side, it can be really hard.

A lot is being able to identify which project you are interested in going super-deep on, because you aren't going to be able to convey to the user what you are trying to do unless it's perfect, and identifying which projects are, "Hey, we would rather get this thing that's 80 percent baked out, because you put it out for a week and we'll know if it's worth spending any more time on." Hone your spidy-skills to determine which project will take more upfront design time. Design is always a really limited resource, so you don't want to waste it on stuff that doesn't need it, at the expense of things that really do. We're always trying to figure out the projects where, instead of having a designer spend a week in Photoshop ahead of time, we can just work with an engineer at a whiteboard for a few hours and come up with something that applies the benefits of design thinking without designing things. We've always been trying to get better at that.

THE EXAMPLE OF TESTING THE SHADES OF BLUE AT GOOGLE IS SORT OF THE QUINTESSENTIAL EXAMPLE OF HOW TO DRIVE DESIGNERS CRAZY. WHAT ARE SOME OF THE TACTICS YOU'VE USED TO HELP YOUR COLLEAGUES UNDERSTAND THE VALUE OF INTUITION AND RESEARCH?

Once you have the ability to A/B test things, you tend to rely on it too much. It's good for some things, but there are certain things that have to be intuition driven. There are certain things that you just know are a bad experience. Yes, it might perform better, but is that something that you feel OK about?

The topic tends to come up most in growth-related activities, like converting users. That's where you end up making something that may work, but likely for a short-term gain. You could potentially undermine the overall experience a user has with the product, which won't be good for you in the long term. You have to be OK taking the hit in the short term because you know something is right.

You should give designers the time and space to uncover, say, three totally different ways to get at this problem. That always goes a long way. People might not necessarily think of three drastically different solutions that you can't get at without going through that process. And this idea and potential solution generation can happen really fast. You can come up with ten quick sketches on how to upload a photo, or whatever it is, and that's something that's harder to do if you are approaching it from an engineering point of view.

After talking to friends who are designer-founders, I think it comes down to what an organization values—what you want to stand behind as your product, what matters, and what you are proud of. Good or thoughtful design used to be a differentiator. Now it's table stakes. If you expect your users to carve out a part of every day or every week to use your product, it has to feel great.

conclusion
the future of product management

Joe is sitting on a beach, drinking a margarita. He's reflecting on the last three years and the success he's had. It's been a wild ride. LiveWell is boasting widespread adoption and great reviews, and the company was just acquired by a large health-club chain. Joe smiles and closes his eyes. He can't wait to sink his teeth into his next project.

In this book, you've learned about the design process. This process focuses on people, celebrates emotional value, and drives optimism through lateral and divergent thinking. You've learned how to build both understanding and empathy with the people who will use your product through a research methodology that requires you to leave your office and spend time with people. You also examined how to translate the things you see and hear into insights, which act as the big rocks of new product innovation. You learned how to tell stories about people achieving their goals and can use your insights to frame those stories. And you learned how to use an emotional value statement as a primary North Star, a goal around which your entire team can rally.

When you view design as a strategic competency, it transcends surface beauty or form. It becomes a way of thinking about problems and people, and a way of working through complexity and ambiguity in order to make our world more engaging. In the future, more and more jobs will leverage this empathetic process of managing ambiguity and driving creativity. I presented the methods in this book in the context of a digital product, but they are equally effective in creating new services, new policies, new business models, new strategies, and new ways of delivering value. The broad applicability of the design process makes it powerful. We are all becoming product managers, and our best process for success is a process of design—a creative process built on a platform of empathy.

notes

INTRODUCTION

1. D. Zax, "A Smart, Sexy—Thermostat?!" *MIT Technology Review*, December 6, 2011, http://www.technologyreview.com/view/426289/a-smart-sexy-thermostat/; S. Kessler, "Nest: The Story Behind the World's Most Beautiful Thermostat," *Mashable*, December 2011, http://mashable.com/2011/12/15/nest-labs-interview/; and "Second-gen Nest Zeroes in on Perfection," CNET, October 2, 2012, http://reviews.cnet.com/appliances/nest-learning-thermostat/4505-17889_7-35179222.html.

2. *PCMag*, May 26, 2011, http://www.pcmag.com/article2/0,2817,2380586,00.asp.

3. N. Robischon, "Square Brings Credit Card Swiping to the Mobile Masses, Starting Today," *Fast Company*, May 11, 2010, http://www.fastcompany.com/1643271/square-brings-credit-card-swiping-mobile-masses-starting-today.

CHAPTER 1

1. R. Martin, "How Successful Leaders Think," *Harvard Business Review*, June 2007.

2. I. Fried, "Apple Bets Consumers are Ready for Cubist Movement," CNET, July 19, 2000, http://news.cnet.com/2100-1040-243373.html.

3. L. Kahney, "Apple Cube: Alive and Selling," *Wired*, July 28, 2003, http://www.wired.com/gadgets/mac/news/2003/07/59764?currentPage=all.

4. I. Fried, "Apple: We Expected to Sell 3 Times More Cubes," CNET, February 1, 2001, http://news.cnet.com/2100-1040-251936.html.

CHAPTER 2

1. S. Pace, *The Global Positioning System: Assessing National Policies* (Santa Monica, CA: RAND, 1995).

2. Raytheon, "Raytheon Company: History," September 27, 2013, http://www.raytheon. com/ourcompany/history/.

3. J. Timmer, "AT&T Squeezes 18Mbps U-verse DSL Out of Last-Mile Copper," ARS Technica, November 6, 2008, http://arstechnica.com/business/2008/11/att-squeezes-18mbps-u-verse-dsl-out-of-last-mile-copper/.

4. Apple, "App Review Guidelines. Apple Developer," 2012, https://developer.apple. com/app-store/review/ for more information.

5. T. Friedman, "Welcome to the 'Sharing Economy,'" *New York Times*, July 20, 2013.

6. R. Lawler, "Uber Moves Deeper into Ride Sharing, Promises to Roll Out Services Where Regulators Have Given 'Tacit Approval,'" *TechCrunch*, April 13, 2013, http:// techcrunch.com/2013/04/12/uber-ride-share-almost-everywhere/.

7. D. Solomon, "City to Heyride: Not So Fast," *Austin Chronicle*, November 30, 2012.

8. R. Lawler, "SideCar Acquires Austin-Based Ride-Sharing Startup Heyride, Will Soon Launch in 7 New Markets," *TechCrunch*, February 14, 2013.

9. "Zappos' 10-Hour Long Customer Service Call Sets Record," *Huffington Post*, December 21, 2012, http://www.huffingtonpost.com/2012/12/21/zappos-10-hour-call_n_2345467.html.

10. D. Reisinger, "WordPress: 72K Blog Posts Exited Tumblr in 1 Hour over Yahoo Deal," CNET, May 20, 2013, http://news.cnet.com/8301-1023_3-57585268-93/wordpress-72k-blog-posts-exited-tumblr-in-1-hour-over-yahoo-deal/.

11. Wikipedia, http://en.wikipedia.org/wiki/AACS_encryption_key_controversy.

12. Stanford, "The Demo," http://sloan.stanford.edu/mousesite/1968Demo.html; and B. Rhodes, "A Brief History of Wearable Computing," MIT Media Laboratory, http://www.media.mit.edu/wearables/lizzy/timeline.html#1981b.

13. B. Buxton, "On Long Noses, Sampling, Synthesis, and Innovation," presentation at UX London, April 19, 2012.

14. J. Lowy, "Virgin America Ranks Best U.S. Airline, United Ranks Worst," *Huffington Post*, April 8, 2013, http://www.huffingtonpost.com/2013/04/08/virgin-america-best-airline_n_3038556.html.

CHAPTER 4

1. J. Norman, interview by author, August 30, 2013.

2. D. Sullivan, "Google Gets a Tag Line: 'Search, Ads & Apps,'" May 11, 2007, http://searchengineland.com/google-gets-a-tag-line-search-ads-apps-11195.

3. M. Kruzeniski, "Poetry & Polemics in Creating Experience," http://www.ixda.org/resources/mike-kruzeniski-poetry-polemics-creating-experience.

4. M. Walsh, "Harnessing the Power of Positive Tension," *Interactions magazine*, 2013.

5. A. Walter, "MailChimp Email Preview Easter Egg," 2010, http://vimeo.com/10981566.

6. C. Chima, "MailChimp Grants Employees 'Permission to Be Creative,'" Fast Co.Create, 2013, http://www.fastcocreate.com/1679207/mailchimp-grants-employees-permission-to-be-creative.

7. A. Walter, interview by author, May 28, 2013.

8. A. Cooper, *The Inmates Are Running the Asylum* (Upper Saddle River, NJ: Pearson Education, 2004).

9. D. Hofstadter, *Surfaces and Essences: Analogy as the Fuel and Fire of Thinking* (New York: Basic Books, 2013).

CHAPTER 5

1. H. Dubberly, interview by author, 2013.

2. N. Group, "Better Tech Support Could Help Decrease Electronics Returns by Nearly 70 Percent, According to NPD," PR Web, August 25, 2009, http://www.prweb.com/printer/2778774.htm.

3. J. Wu, interview by author, 2013.

4. F. S. Fitzgerald, "The Crack Up," *Esquire*, 1936, http://www.esquire.com/features/the-crack-up.

5. D. Merkoski, interview by author, 2013.

CHAPTER 6

1. P. Smalley, interview by author, May 2, 2013.

2. J. M. Spool, "The $300 Million Button," User Interface Engineering, January 14, 2009, http://www.uie.com/articles/three_hund_million_button/.

index

patterns and anomalies identified in,
87–88
risk in interpreting, 43
technology acceptance and, 37–38,
42, 48–50
value-goal statement for, 51–53, 52t
what-if questions used in, 55–58
Smalley, Preston, 200
soul of product, 114, 121–122
specs, 66
spreadsheet, for transcript of behavioral
insights, 86
Square, 2, 70
stakeholders
Chou interview on, 106
product-market fit and, 36
Starbucks, 3
storytelling
design strategy as form of, 115–116
Elman interview on, 68–69
Gebbia at Airbnb interview on, 30–31
hero maps and, 154–156
product road maps for, 185–187
strategy. *See* design strategy; market
strategy; product strategy
suppliers, and product-market fit, 36
support tickets, 204
sustainability, 28
sweating details, 190–191

taxicab industry, 40, 57
teams
celebrating victories on, 204–205
Chou interview on, 104–105
Gebbia at Airbnb interview on, 30–31
product vision artifacts and, 162–164
Rainert interview on, 206
short-circuiting debate in, 199–200
teaching and evangelizing for,
196–198
tear sheets, of visual design, 193–196, 197f
technology
cultural attitude shifts and, 48–50
designers in human-to-human
interactions and, 21
design process centered on, 17
design strategy and, 114, 115–116, 127
product management by design and, 19
product-market fit and readiness for,
37–38, 42, 48–50
Telstra telecommunications company,
130, 132

textbook publishing industry, 164, 167,
169–171
Textbook Renter, 170
thinking artifacts, 51, 55, 156
thinking out loud, during observations for
behavioral insights, 81
3D printing, 49
Thuuz sports service, 130–131
Tide brand detergent, 165–166, 174
timing, and product-market fit, 38, 69
tracking defects, 192
transcription of behavioral insights, 85–86
trends
collaborative consumption and,
40–41
product-market fit and, 39, 40
Tribe.net online community, 97–98,
108, 109
Trilogy enterprise software company,
96–97
TrueCar car buying website, 135
trust, 192
Tumblr online community, 46, 47, 101,
102–03, 110
Twitter, 45, 59, 61, 64, 67–68, 70, 101–02,
113, 121, 180

Uber ride-sharing application, 41, 70
uncertainty, what-if questions on, 55–58
understanding, and behavioral insights,
72, 74–75, 76
Union Square Ventures, 95–96, 98,
100–102, 106
United Airlines, 52–53
usability, 3, 18, 28, 105, 119, 121, 153, 191
usability tests, 81. *See also* observations for
behavioral insights
usability tracking system, 192
user behavior. *See also* behavioral insights
data on, 203–204
user-centered design process, 16–17
user-centered product management,
18–19, 20, 36
user experience
Gebbia at Airbnb interview on, 26–34
researcher for, 212–213
user interface
computer mouse introduction and,
48, 49
design strategy and, 117
Elman interview on, 63–64
as signals, 42–43

about the author

Jon Kolko is Vice President of Consumer Design at Blackboard Inc. He joined Blackboard with the acquisition of MyEdu, a start-up focused on helping students succeed in college and find internships and jobs. He is also the founder and Director of Austin Center for Design. His work focuses on bringing the power of design to social enterprises, with an emphasis on entrepreneurship. He has worked extensively with both start-ups and *Fortune* 500 companies, and he's most interested in humanizing educational technology.

Prior to Blackboard, Jon was Executive Director of Design Strategy at Thinktiv, a venture accelerator in Austin, Texas, and both Principal Designer and Associate Creative Director at frog design, a global innovation firm. He has been a Professor of Interaction Design and Industrial Design at the Savannah College of Art and Design, where he was instrumental in building these programs at the undergraduate and graduate levels. Jon has also held the role of director for the Interaction Design Association (IxDA) and editor-in-chief of *Interactions* magazine. He is regularly asked to participate in high-profile conferences and juried design events, including the 2013 Cooper Hewitt National Design Awards. He has taught at the University of Texas at Austin, the Center for Design Studies of Monterrey, in Mexico, and Malmö University, in Sweden.

Jon is the author of three other books: *Thoughts on Interaction Design, Exposing the Magic of Design: A Practitioner's Guide to the Methods and Theory of Synthesis*, and *Wicked Problems: Problems Worth Solving*.